CHOOSING YOUR BIBLE

Bible Translation Differences

Edward D. Andrews

CHOOSING YOUR BIBLE

Bible Translation Differences

Edward D. Andrews

Christian Publishing House

Cambridge, Ohio

Christian Publishing House

Professional Christian Publishing of the Good News

CHOOSING YOUR BIBLE: Bible Translation Differences by Edward D. Andrews

ISBN-13: 978-1-945757-68-6

ISBN-10: 1-945757-68-X

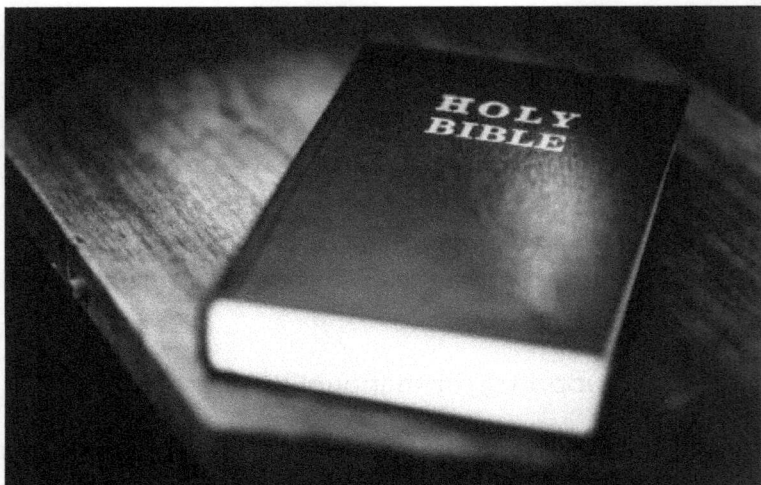

Table of Contents

CHAPTER 1 The King James Version after 400 Years: Looking Back, Looking Forward

Leland Ryken

Wheaton College

The King James Version has reached the milestone of the 400th anniversary of its first publication. Academic and religious conferences, museum displays, books and articles, and commemorative editions of the KJV have exploded in such quantity that 2011 can confidently be declared the year of the King James Bible. Although King James I granted a Puritan request for a new Bible translation with the sneering put-down that he had never seen the Bible well translated into English, a spirit of benediction fell in the process of translation and the book that resulted.

The King James Version is a book of superlatives. For three centuries, when English-speaking people spoke of "the Bible," they meant the King James Version. The King James Bible is the all-time best seller among English language books, and according to David Daniell, in his magisterial book The Bible in English; the KJV is still the best-selling book worldwide. The King James Bible is the most quoted English book, the most widely read, the most printed, and the most influential. It is no wonder that Gordon Campbell claims in his book Bible: The Story of the King James Version 1611-2011 that the King James Version is "the most important book in the English language."

The King James Version in the Church

We can divide the influence of the King James Bible into the two spheres of its influence in (1) the church and

(2) the culture of England and America. From the time of its publication until the middle of the twentieth century, the King James Bible was the only major Bible in use among Christian individuals, families, and churches.

I myself grew up in that milieu. When at the age of nine my parents gave me a Bible with my name embossed on it, it was a King James Bible. I memorized verses from the King James Bible at home, school, and church. Twice every Sunday the King James Version was read and expounded from the pulpit. I heard the King James Bible read after every meal, three times a day. My experience was doubtless replicated by millions of English-speaking Christians through the centuries.

When we pick up Bible commentaries from the past like Matthew Henry's commentary, we find that the authors who wrote them do not even tell us what translation of the Bible they have used (in obvious contrast to commentaries published in recent decades). It was simply understood that the author of a commentary had used the King James Version as the base text. If we read the sermons of the towering preachers of the past— Jonathan Edwards, Charles Spurgeon, Billy Graham—the quotations from the Bible are from the King James Version. When we step into a church in England or America that has Bible verses on the walls, we hardly need to ask what translation is represented: it is the King James Version.

The Cultural Influence in the King James Version

Until the middle of the twentieth century, the Bible formed the universally accepted frame of reference for English-speaking cultures. Here, too, it was axiomatic that the King James Version was the Bible in view. In my book The Legacy of the King James Bible, I survey the spheres of culture where the King James Version was preeminent for over three centuries They include public discourse (such as presidential addresses and courtroom speeches), education, music, visual art, and literature.

One of my favorite pieces of research for my book was public inscriptions that bear texts from the King James Version. During my years at the University of Oregon I could look up every time I entered the library and read, "Ye shall know the truth, and the truth shall make you free" (John 8:32, KJV). Every year two million visitors file past the cracked Liberty Bell in Philadelphia and read, "Proclaim LIBERTY through all the Land unto all the Inhabitants thereof" (Leviticus 25:10, KJV). Inscribed on the "Isaiah wall" across the street from the United Nations headquarters in New York City is Isaiah 2:4: "They shall beat their swords into plowshares, and their spears into pruning hooks...."

But these inscriptions are merely a shorthand index to the influence of the King James Version in culture. Even if every copy of the King James Version were to vanish suddenly, the King James Bible would live on in the music, visual art, and literature of the English-speaking world.

It is right that the King James Version is being honored in many corners of England and America in this anniversary year. Regardless of what English translation one uses today, Christians should celebrate the fact that the King James Bible is the most influential English-language book of all time. Conversely, the sneering put-downs of the King James Version by people who prefer dynamic equivalent and colloquial translations are inappropriate. Instead of gloating over the proliferation of modern translations, we should take stock of what was lost with the proliferation that began in the middle of the twentieth century. What was lost was a common Bible and all of the advantages that resulted from having a single Bible that English-speaking Christendom used. Biblical illiteracy has accompanied the eclipse of the King James Bible.

The King James Version Today

The remainder of this chapter will cast an eye to the future and ask what functions the King James Version can serve in a day when it is only one of a dozen prominent English Bibles. But before I look forward, I want to take stock of the King James Version today.

First, the rumors of the demise of the King James Version have been greatly exaggerated (to cite the comment made by Mark Twain when he read a newspaper account claiming that he was dead). If we consult the current sales of English Bibles, we will find that the King James Version is either second or third on the list. Then if we look at websites related to the King James Bible, we find many churches and schools that remain loyal users of the King James Version. People who use a modern translation (as I myself do) have an unwarranted tendency to assume that everyone else, too, has abandoned the King James Version for a modern translation.

Additionally, in the literary sphere, the King James Version continues to reign unchallenged. Within my own guild of literary authors and scholars, the number of people who use anything other than the King James Version in their literary endeavors is statistically insignificant. Similarly, any study of art and music from the past that is rooted in the King James Bible requires that teachers and students use the same translation that is woven into the fabric of the art and music. In fact, every time we read a sermon, a religious document, a novel, a poem, a courtroom speech, a political speech from the seventeenth century through the middle of the twentieth century that quotes from the Bible, the King James Version lives on in the present.

Looking Forward

I have already provided several answers to the question of what we can expect for the KJV in the future. We can expect thousands and probably millions of English-speaking readers to continue to read the King James Bible. We can expect literary authors and to lesser extent musical composers to weave the King James Version into their artistic works. In addition, scholars who teach and write about the literature, art, and music of the past have no good alternative to using the KJV in their scholarship.

My subject in the rest of this essay is to explore the continuing usefulness of the KJV as a model for English Bible translation today. My starting point is a comment that Alister McGrath makes on the last page of his book entitled In the Beginning: The Story of the King James Bible and How It Changed a Nation, a Language, and a Culture. "The true heirs of the King James translators," writes McGrath, "are those who continue their task today, not those who declare it to have been definitively concluded in 1611." I interpret McGrath's phrase "those who continue their task today" to mean "those who perpetuate the translation philosophy and style of the King James Version." I think that the statement is preeminently true of the English Standard Version.

There are two dimensions to an English Bible, and accordingly two spheres in which the King James Version can serve as a reliable guide to modern translators. One is the content of a translation, what the translators put in front of the reading public as representing what the authors of the Bible wrote. The second is the style in which an English translation is embodied. Beginning in the middle of the twentieth century, all translation committees have faced a need to choose between perpetuating the King James tradition and repudiating it.

I want to start my projection into the future by elaborating on my previous statement that modern translation committees face a fork in the road at which they must make a choice. The King James Bible itself was a synthesis of a series of six English Bible translations that had appeared during the sixteenth century, starting with William Tyndale. Unlike what prevails with many modern translations, the King James translators did not wish to be innovative and original. They did not view the preceding translations as rivals but as contributors to their own effort. The entire sixteenth-century project was based on a communal understanding of knowledge in which successive translators viewed themselves as inheriting a great tradition, improving it, and then passing it on.

The preface to the King James Version makes this principle of continuity with the existing tradition explicit. In a famous statement in the prefatory document entitled "The Translators to the Reader," we read, "Truly (good Christian Reader) we never thought from the beginning, that we should need to make a new Translation, nor yet to make of a bad one a good one, . . . but to make a good one better, or out of many good ones, one principal good one, not to be excepted against."

This principle of perpetuating the great tradition from Tyndale through the King James Version is one way in which the KJV continues to exert an influence even among translators and readers who cast their lot with a modern translation. The prefaces to three modern translations explicitly align those translations with what is variously called the King James tradition, the Tyndale-King James legacy, and the classic mainstream of English Bible translations. The three translations that consciously perpetuate the principles of the King James tradition are the Revised Standard Version, the New King James Version, and the English Standard Version.

By contrast, adherents of dynamic equivalent translations and colloquial translations either distance themselves from the King James tradition or repudiate it. One will look in vain for any statement of continuity with the KJV in the prefaces to these translations. The reason is obvious: the translators who produced these translations do not agree with the translation philosophy or the stylistic norms of the King James tradition. I turn now to these two subjects.

Perpetuating the Translation Philosophy of the King James Version

The King James translators did not consciously choose the translation philosophy that today goes by such names as verbal equivalence, essentially literal, or formal equivalence. Starting with Tyndale and running through the middle of the twentieth century, this was the only view of Bible of translation that held any genuine credence. Tyndale actually coined as many as two thousand English words in an effort to render in English what the biblical authors had written. Examples include intercession, atonement, peacemaker, and Passover. Not until the rise of dynamic equivalence was there any widespread doubt that the goal of English Bible translation was to take the reader as close as possible to the very words of the biblical authors.

The King James Version accepted this premise without reservation. The translators found an equivalent English word or phrase for everything that was in the original text—but not more than was in the original text. They were so scrupulous about keeping the record straight regarding the original text that they followed the practice of the Geneva Bible of putting into italics words that had been added for the sake of intelligibility or fluency in English.

As we look toward the future, then, we can say that the King James Version lives on among modern translations that likewise give readers an equivalent English word or phrase for everything that is in the original. The true significance of this is blunted if we simply quote from an essentially literal modern translation. To see the true significance, we need to set a literal translation alongside dynamic equivalent translations. The King James model lives on when a modern translation renders the last verse of Psalm 87 as "all my springs are in you." It dies when non-literal translations render it as "I too am from Jerusalem"(CEV) or "all good things come from Jerusalem"(NCV) or "in Zion is the source of all our blessings."(GNB)

Honoring the King James Style

Content is one-half of an English Bible translation and style is the other half. Style refers to the vocabulary and sentence structure through which the translation embodies the content. What role can the King James Version serve for future English Bible translation? That question is easily answered: the King James Version lives on as a stylistic influence in the branch of English Bible translations that position themselves in the King James lineage, also called the classic mainstream of English Bible translation.

Since I believe that the English Standard Version (ESV) is truest to the King James style, though, in updated language and grammar, I will take my illustrations from it. Right in the preface, we can see the claim that the ESV perpetuates the style of the King James Version. The preface claims that the ESV retains the "enduring language" of the King James tradition. That is a virtual code language for "the dignity, beauty, and elegance that is a hallmark of the King James Bible." The adjectives that we find in the prefaces of colloquial translations are "fresh" and "innovative" and "common," but emphatically not "enduring." Elsewhere the preface to the ESV speaks of the "simplicity, beauty, and dignity of expression" that it carries on from the King James Version and Revised Standard Version.

It is not immediately apparent what descriptors to use when describing the King James style, but the words elegant (not to be equated with eloquent), dignified, and beautiful are indisputably accurate. The King James translators and their modern heirs do not reduce the Bible to the level of conversational or colloquial discourse as it prevails in the dormitory or the local coffee shop. At this point, it is relevant to observe that the Bible in its original form is a primarily literary book. Literature always does things with language and syntax that elevate a statement above informal conversation.

The key to the style of the King James Version and the English Standard Version is that it is elegant without being stilted. The actual vocabulary is often simple, but the effect is majestic. Since any choice of a specimen is somewhat arbitrary, I will simply select the famous statement from Jesus found in Luke 11:9-10: "Ask, and it will be give to you; seek, and you will find; knock, and it will be opened to you. For everyone who asks receives, and the one who seeks finds, and to the one who knocks it will be opened" (ESV). The vocabulary is simple, but the patterns of parallelism and antithesis raise the statement far above the chatter at the bus stop.

Summary

The King James Version is far from dead. It lives on as a cultural presence, especially (but not only) in the culture that comes to us from the past. It lives on among readers and churches that use it as their primary Bible. It lives on in modern translations like the ESV that perpetuate the translation philosophy and stylistic norms of the King James Version.

CHAPTER 2 William Tyndale's Plowboy Reconsidered

Leland Ryken

Wheaton College

This essay is a historical study. That may seem anomalous in a journal devoted to current translation issues and practices, so a word of explanation is in order. One of the functions of inquiring into the history of English Bible translation is that it can clarify the essential principles of Bible translation. When the issues are distanced from us in time, we can see some things more clearly because they are unclouded by contemporary crosswinds.

More important than the clarifying power of distance, though, is the authority that attaches to historical precedents. This authority may or not be completely valid, but it is a fact that in the current debate between rival translation philosophies an appeal to historical precedents is considered important. Both literal translators and dynamic equivalent and colloquial translators probe the past to find examples of their own preferred style of translation.

The current debate about William Tyndale

It is obvious that we live in a day of debunking. On the Bible translation scene, advocates of colloquial English Bible translations regularly and rigorously debunk the King James Version. In turn, it has become common for these debunkers to attempt to drive a wedge between the King James Version and William Tyndale's translation work nearly a century earlier.

More specifically, the claim is made that the King James translators spoiled Tyndale by refining his style.

Eugene Peterson, the author of The Message, has, of course, led the charge, but he is not alone. Predictably, the claim is made that Tyndale produced a colloquial translation while the King James translation is elegant. Peterson claims that the King James translators "desecrated language upwards" [Eat This Book (Grand Rapids: Eerdmans, 2006), 162].

The most famous statement that Tyndale made about Bible translation, next to his dying prayer that God would open the king of England's eyes, is a comment that he made about wanting the plowboy to know the Bible better than the Catholic priests. I will quote the statement shortly and then analyze it, but as a lead-in to that, I need to note that translators in what I call the "modernizing" camp claim that Tyndale in a single utterance endorsed (1) a colloquial style for an English Bible, (2) an uneducated reader as the assumed audience for an English Bible, and (3) a dynamic equivalent philosophy of translation (buttressed, of course, by a few famous examples from Tyndale's actual translation). My thesis in this article is that Tyndale's plowboy statement has been extravagantly misinterpreted and that none of the three conclusions I listed in the previous sentence is warranted.

Exactly what did Tyndale say?

Tyndale's plowboy statement is recounted in John Foxe's Book of Martyrs. The context of the statement itself disproves the use to which modernizing translators put it. Tyndale had uttered the statement before he had even begun his work of translating the Bible. The occasion of the statement was not Bible translation per se. Instead, the statement occurred as part of the debate about whether the pope or the Bible is the ultimate authority for religious belief and practice.

Upon graduating from Oxford University, Tyndale returned to his native Gloucestershire and assumed the position as a schoolmaster in the Catholic household of Sir John Walsh. Tyndale was an early Reformer whose views brought him into heated debates with the local clergy. Tyndale was appalled at the ignorance of the Catholic clergy. Additionally, he was convinced of the Protestant doctrine of sola scriptura on the question of religious authority. I propose that these two things, the biblical ignorance of the clergy and the question of biblical authority, are the context for Tyndale's statement about the plowboy.

We can hear these two themes of biblical ignorance among the clergy and the authority of Bible in the statement that I now quote:

> There dwelt not far off a certain doctor, that he been chancellor to a bishop, who had been of old, familiar acquaintance with Master Tyndale, and favored him well; unto whom Master Tyndale went and opened his mind upon divers questions of the Scripture: for to him he durst be bold to disclose his heart. Unto whom the doctor said, "Do you not know that the pope is very Antichrist, whom the Scripture speaketh of? But beware what you say; for if you shall be perceived to be of that opinion, it will cost you your life."   Not long after, Master Tyndale happened to be in the company of a certain divine, recounted for a learned man, and, in communing and disputing with him, he drove him to that issue, that the said great doctor burst out into these blasphemous words, "We were better to be without God's laws than the pope's." Master Tyndale, hearing this, full of godly zeal, and not bearing that blasphemous saying, replied, "I defy the pope, and all his laws;" and added, "If God spared him life, ere many years he would cause a boy that driveth the plough to know more of the Scripture than he did." The

grudge of the priests increasing still more and more against Tyndale, they never ceased barking and rating at him, and laid many things sorely to his charge, saying that he was a heretic.

We should note first what is not going on here. The statement about the plowboy is not a comment about Tyndale's preferred style for an English Bible. It is not a designation of teenage farm boys as a target audience for a niche Bible. In fact, the account does not even mention translation of the Bible into English. Foxe's account makes it clear that the subject of debate at this early stage in Tyndale's career was the question of papal authority vs. scriptural authority. When the priest asserted a strong view of papal authority and denigrated the authority of the Bible, Tyndale responded by making an implied case for the Bible as the authority for Christian belief and conduct. We should not overlook Foxe's follow-up comment about "the grudge of the priests." The plowboy statement is part of a debate with Catholic priests over papal authority, not on the style of an English Bible.

Therefore, what did Tyndale mean in his famous plowboy statement? First, he implicitly asserted the right of the laity to the Bible. The plowboy is a representative of the whole of English society. Tyndale's statement is not a comment about English style but about how widely Tyndale wanted the English Bible to be disseminated in English society. Even the humble working class should have access to the Bible.

Secondly, Tyndale was making a statement about how much of the Bible he wanted the laity to know. His statement, to quote again, is "that he would cause a boy that driveth the plough to know more of the Scripture than [the priest] did." The typical priest knew the snatches of Scripture that were embedded in the liturgy, the mass, and choral music, and he would have known it in Latin.

What I most want to challenge is the view that Tyndale was an ally of what I call modernizing and colloquializing English Bibles that have proliferated since the middle of the twentieth century. Whatever we conclude about Tyndale's preferred style in English translation is something we need to deduce from his actual translation, not from his statement about the plowboy.

Conclusion

Tyndale's plowboy statement is a virtual Rorschach inkblot [interpretation] in which modern translators see what they themselves believe about English Bible translation. In turn, Tyndale is such a towering figure that if one can claim him for one's side in the translation wars, it is, in fact, a victory. I submit that Tyndale's plowboy statement should not be allowed to lend any support whatever to dynamic equivalent and colloquial translations. Exactly where Tyndale stood on questions of essentially literal vs. dynamic equivalence and dignified vs. colloquial style needs to rest on his actual translation of the Bible.

CHAPTER 3 The Bible Translation Debate

Leland Ryken

Wheaton College

UNTIL THE MIDDLE OF THE TWENTIETH CENTURY, all major English Bible translations were based on the premise that the goal of Bible translation is to take the reader as close as possible to the words that the biblical authors actually wrote. William Tyndale, the fountainhead of English Bible translation, even made up English words like intercession, atonement, scapegoat, and Passover in order to do justice to the very words of the biblical text.

Equally striking are the italicized words in the King James Version. Surely many English readers are mystified by the italicizing of words and phrases in the KJV. Following the lead of the Geneva Bible (1560), the King James translators were so scrupulous about keeping the record clear as to what the biblical authors actually wrote that they italicized words that the translators added for the sake of clarity or fluency in English. By contrast, modern dynamic equivalent translators hope to keep readers in the dark regarding changes that have been made to the original. If that seems like a doubtful statement, I will just adduce the example of a colleague of mine who was given permission to produce an interlinear version of the NIV New Testament. A high-ranking person in the publishing house expressed surprise that this permission had been granted since it would show at once how many words in the NIV have no corresponding word in the Greek original.

Exactly What Happened in the Middle of the Twentieth-Century?

All major translations before the rise of dynamic equivalent translations were based on the principle of literal translation, also known as verbal equivalence. This translation philosophy strives to give an equivalent English word or phrase for all words found in the original text of the Bible. The goal is to convey everything that it is in the original, but not more than is in the original or less than is there.

The new translation philosophy is called dynamic equivalence, but that designation is very inadequate to cover all that modernizing translations actually do. In fact, equivalence is not usually, what these translations give. Usually, they give a substitution or replacement for what the original says. Additionally, dynamic equivalent translators omit material from material in the original and add to it. Dynamic equivalent translators feel no compulsion to reproduce in English the words that the biblical authors wrote. In fact, the prefaces to these translations, as well as surrounding published materials and interviews, hold verbal equivalence up to scorn. These prefaces and translators are bold to claim that a translation that departs from the words of the biblical authors is often more accurate than translations that reproduce the words of the original text.

Are my claims really true? I will give an example of each of the three common maneuvers of dynamic equivalent translators.

Omitting Material from the Bible

The most plentiful parts of the Bible where this is done is passages with figurative language. In 1 Corinthians 16:9, Paul speaks metaphorically of "a wide door" that has "opened" to him (ESV). Dynamic equivalent translators who believe that modern readers cannot understand metaphors simply remove the wide door from sight: "a good opportunity" (New Century Version); "a wonderful opportunity" (Contemporary English Version); "a real opportunity" (Good News Bible). As all of this license unfolds before us, we need to ask, Who gave us the metaphor of the wide door in the first place? The answer should be, The writers of the Bible writing under the inspiration of the Holy Spirit.

Offering a Substitute for What Is in the Bible

The omission of material from the original text is often accompanied by a substitution for what a biblical author wrote. In Psalm 73, the poet recalls his crisis of faith in metaphoric terms: "my steps had nearly slipped" (v. 2b, ESV). Several dynamic equivalent translations give us a substitute for the image of slipping steps: "I had almost lost my faith" (New Century Version); "my faith was almost gone" (Good News Bible). As one expert on Bible translation exclaims, "This is not translation at all but merely replacement."

Adding Commentary to what the Biblical Authors Wrote

Dynamic equivalent translators incessantly add commentary to what the original text gives us. Of course, the reader has no clue as to where the original text of the Bible ends and the commentary of the translators begin. In Psalm 23:5a, David writes, "You anoint my head with oil." There is no dispute that this is what the original text says. But dynamic equivalent translators feel an overpowering urge to add commentary beyond the biblical text: "You welcome me as a guest, anointing my head with oil" (NLT). Unless you can read the Hebrew original or have the good fortune to be familiar with a literal translation, you cannot answer the question of where the original text ends, and the translator's commentary begins. Of course, you should be able to trust your English Bible not to mislead you.

Why Would Translators Do These Things?

Why do translators feel free to engage in the kind of license I have noted? There are several answers. First, Bible translation took a wrong turn when the concept of a target audience became enthroned. This concept envisions an audience of limited linguistic and theological abilities. The almost universally accepted criterion of dynamic equivalent translations is a reader with the linguistic and theological comprehension of a sixth-grader. With this target audience firmly ensconced, the entire translation is then slanted toward the assumed abilities of this audience. I agree with the verdict of Dr. John McArthur, who in an endorsement of one of my books spoke of translators who are more concerned with the human audience than the divine author of the Bible is.

Additionally, the entire dynamic equivalent enterprise is based on the premise that the Bible is an inadequate book that needs correction. All we need to do is read the prefaces of these translations and observe what the translators have done to see that the translators believe that they can communicate better than the biblical authors did. The biblical authors used metaphors, but modern readers cannot understand metaphoric language. The biblical authors used theological language, but the theological language is beyond modern readers. Etc., etc. The view of biblical authors that emerge from this branch of Bible translation is that they are inept and in need of correction. It is no wonder that half a century of dynamic equivalent translations has made the following formula omnipresent in evangelical circles: "now what the biblical author was trying to say is ..."

What Is at Stake in the Current Debate?

Two things chiefly are at stake in the current debate between the rival translations philosophies. One is whether we can trust our English Bibles. I propose that we cannot trust dynamic equivalent translations to put us in contact with the Bible that God inspired the human authors to write. What is the assumption (completely legitimate) that we all make when we hold a book in our hands? Surely that the publisher has put into print the words that the author wrote. Dynamic equivalent translations consistently betray that trust.

Additionally, English readers need to choose between the actual Bible that God inspired his authors to write or a substitute for that Bible. I resonate completely with an emailer who wrote to me that he was raised on a literal Bible, gravitated to a dynamic equivalent translation through peer pressure, and returned to a literal translation after reading one of my books. His parting point was "it was as though someone had given me my Bible back."

When dynamic equivalence swept the field half a century ago, people were so intoxicated by the exciting new view of Bible translation that they did not pay attention to what was actually happening. The time has come for sober reality. I would urge readers of the English Bible to practice what an advertising slogan of several years ago advocated: Accept no substitute.

CHAPTER 4 Differences in Bible Translations

Leland Ryken

Wheaton College

Interviewed by Christian Publishing House

Prior to 2001, Dr. Leland Ryken, a professor of English at Wheaton College in Wheaton, Illinois, served on the translation committee as their literary sty ist for the 2001—English Standard Version. He has penned numerous books on the different theories of Bible Translation: such as *The Word of God in English* and *Understanding English Bible Translation*. Christian Publishing House has posted several articles in defense of the literal translation being the preferred Bible for study and research, as well as daily reading and memorization, having often referred to Ryken's books. In fact, he has penned numerous articles for our magazine. In the last seven decades, dynamic equivalent (thought-for-thought) translation advocates have flooded the market with easy to read Bible translations that focus on the reader, not the text, which has literally threatened the integrity of God's Word, and Ryken, has been at the forefront of defending the arguments the dynamic equivalent advocates have raised. Critics have accused him of misleading the reader by not giving all the facts—being unbalanced or subjective in his views—as he is clouded by his personal opinions. Others claim that his reasoning is not rational. Bible Translation

Magazine has interviewed Professor Ryken to learn why his books and articles have caused such a stir.

Below is the conversation Bible Translation Magazine (BTM) had with Dr. Ryken:

CPH: *What is the goal of Bible translation?*

Leland Ryken: The goal of Bible translation is to take readers as close as possible to the actual words that the biblical authors wrote. The translation process that this viewpoint produces is called *verbal equivalence*, which means that every word in the original Hebrew or Greek text is rendered by an *equivalent* or corresponding English word or phrase. The goal of Bible translation is to be transparent to the original text—to see as clearly as possible what the biblical authors actually wrote.

CPH: *What is the process of Bible translation?*

Leland Ryken: Bible translation starts by ascertaining what Hebrew or Greek manuscript family comes closest to what the biblical authors wrote. Since no copies of the original manuscripts exist, this first step is not as easy as one would hope. Secondly, there is the lexical question of what the words in the Hebrew and Greek texts meant when the authors wrote. Thirdly, translators need to determine the most accurate English words and phrases by which to render the Hebrew and Greek words. This includes (a) avoiding English words that have the wrong meanings and connotations, and (b) choosing the most accurate English words and phrases.

CPH: *Why is there always a need for new translations?*

Leland Ryken: The need for new translations arises from the nature of language. Language is always in the process of changing. New words enter the vocabulary of every language. Words that are no longer regularly used become obsolete and archaic. Often the meanings of words change. Even fashions in syntax (the order of items in a sentence) can change. Eventually, these changes produce a situation in which evolving language moves out from under every translation.

CPH: *What is the basic history of the English Bible?*

Leland Ryken: Before I note the landmark Bible translations, I need to say something about the philosophy of translation that dominated English Bible translation from the beginning to the middle of the twentieth century. No major translation between Tyndale's New Testament of 1526 and the RSV of 1952 deviated from the view that the goal of English Bible translation is to provide a corresponding English word or phrase for every word in the Hebrew or Greek texts of the Bible. Tyndale coined many English words in order to render exactly what the Hebrew and Greek texts contained. The history of English Bible translation as we know it began with William Tyndale. Five translations stand between Tyndale and the King James Version of 1611. The most important of them was the Geneva Bible of 1560. The King James Version then completely dominated the scene until the middle of the twentieth century, when a new translation philosophy known as dynamic equivalence swept the field, though of course there remained advocates of essentially literal translation. After half a century of dominance by dynamic equivalence, the pendulum began to swing back in the direction of verbal equivalence at the turn of the century.

CPH: *What are the differences among an interlinear translation, a literal translation, a dynamic equivalent translation, and a paraphrase?*

Leland Ryken: Those four categories name the continuum from literal to free. An interlinear translation is completely literal concerning both vocabulary and syntax. An essentially literal translation gives an English equivalent for every word in the original, resorting to a substitute only when a literal rendering makes no sense. Dynamic equivalent translators feel no obligation to find an English equivalent for every word in the original Hebrew and Greek texts; if the text says "he anoints my head with oil," a dynamic equivalent translation might read "he treats me as an honored guest." Paraphrases often bear little resemblance to what the biblical authors wrote (for example, the statement in Psalm 19 that God's law is "sweeter than honey" becomes "you'll like it better than strawberries in spring" (*The Message*).

CPH: *What is the difference between what a text says and what a text means?*

Leland Ryken: What a text *says* is what the author wrote, rendered into the best English equivalent. Translators divide on the question of what the text *means*. Essentially literal translators assume that a biblical author meant what he said, so if they give an English equivalent of the words of the original author, they have also stated the author's meaning. Dynamic equivalent translators operate on the premise that meaning exists independent of the words of the original author. The most helpful way of understanding this is that dynamic equivalent translators feel free to add the activities of a commentator or interpreter to the task of translation. That is really the crux of the difference between the rival translation philosophies. I myself believe that it is inaccurate to call a dynamic equivalent Bible a translation; it is a translation plus a commentary plus the product a heavy editorial hand. To illustrate, Philippians 4:1 contains the phrase "my joy and crown." Essentially literal translators believe that those words contain what the author *meant*. Dynamic equivalent translators abandon the words of the original ("joy and crown") and substitute an exposition of the original text: "how happy you make me, and how proud I am of you" (Good News Bible).

CPH: *Those who favor dynamic equivalence say that "all translation is interpretation." Is this true?*

Leland Ryken: The motto that "all translation is interpretation" is the most abused formula in translation, and a moratorium should be called on its use. All translation is *lexical* interpretation, that is, deciding what English word or phrase best expresses the Hebrew or Greek word in the original text. However, this is not what dynamic equivalent translators chiefly have in mind. What they mean by the phrase is that all translators add commentary to what the Hebrew and Greek texts say. This is patently untrue of essentially literal translations.

CPH: *At what point does a translation infringe on the intention of the author?*

Leland Ryken: Let me begin by describing the history of dynamic equivalence. When Eugene Nida's new philosophy became the norm in the middle of the twentieth century, the very newness of the venture served as a curb on taking excessive liberty with the biblical text. The original NIV of 1978 is a conservative version of dynamic equivalence. In passing, I will say that despite the fact the original NIV is a relatively mild form of dynamic equivalence, I lay a lot of blame on the NIV for having gotten the direction of modern Bible translation set in the wrong direction. Once the NIV made dynamic equivalence "mainstream," we can trace an arc of increasing departure from what the original authors wrote in this family of Bible translations. As I look at this arc of increasing distance from the Hebrew and Greek texts, I infer that the quest to be new and different became part of the picture. Successive waves of translators seem to have set out to see how innovative (and in some cases daring) they could be. The ultimate terminus of this is, of course, Eugene Peterson's *The Message*.

To return to the original question, I believe that the moment translators adopt dynamic equivalence as their methodology they have infringed on the biblical authors' intention. Surely, the biblical writers wrote what they intended to write (and us to read). I have often wondered how dynamic equivalent translators would respond if others did with their scholarly writings what these translators do with the biblical authors. I think they would go into orbit.

CPH: *What are some liberties that dynamic equivalent translators take?*

Leland Ryken: They are well documented in both the practice of dynamic equivalent translators and in their statements of philosophy. Here are the liberties that dynamic equivalent translators regularly take:

(1) replace what the original authors wrote with something else (e.g., where the text says "establish the work of our hands," dynamic equivalent translations substitute "let all go well for us");

(2) change figurative statements into direct statements (again a substitution);

(3) add interpretive commentary to what the biblical authors wrote, so readers do not know what was in the original and what was added;

(4) make the style of the English Bible contemporary and colloquial;

(5) reduce the vocabulary level of the original text;

(6) bring masculine gender references into line with modern feminist preferences. In all these ways, dynamic equivalent translations give the public a substitute Bible. I would also assert that the original authors of the Bible *had the resources to state their content the way dynamic equivalent translators state it*, but instead, they stated it as we find in the original texts of the Bible. Dynamic equivalent translators take a condescending view of the authors of the Bible, treating them like inept writers who couldn't state things accurately and therefore need correction.

CPH: *What can you say about dynamic equivalence and the "dumbing down" in American culture?*

Leland Ryken: Dynamic equivalence is a particular manifestation of the whole drift of American culture during that past half-century. As a culture, we have been conducting an experiment in reducing expectations and standards. I will note in passing that the stylistic level of easy-reading Bibles is exactly the same as what has happened to Christian music and church services. When we consult the prefaces to dynamic equivalent translations, we find that the translators are explicit about the assumed low level of linguistic and intellectual level of their readers. The sixth-grade threshold is widely accepted in these prefaces. The logical conclusion is that readers cannot be educated beyond a sixth-grade level. I would raise the question, In what other areas of life are we content with a sixth-grade level of attainment?

CPH: *Has the dumbing down of Bible translations produced the well-attested biblical illiteracy that we find in the church and in the culture at large?*

Leland Ryken: Some of the blame can be laid at the feet of easy-reading translations. When I read these translations and (even more), hear them read in public, I feel a great letdown and say to myself that such a Bible does not capture my heart and allegiance. A translation that reads like the chatter at the corner coffee shop is given the type of credibility that the chatter is given. But quite apart from that, we need to acknowledge the damage done by the proliferation of Bible translations. With so many contradictory renditions of the biblical text, the public has lost confidence that we can actually know what the Bible says. It is an easy step from this skepticism to an indifference about what the Bible says.

CPH: *What responsibility lies with the reader?*

Leland Ryken: Readers should aspire to what is excellent. They should refuse to read a substitute Bible.

They should want a Bible that calls them to their higher selves—or to something higher than their current level of attainment. I was raised on the King James Version. As a youngster, I did not suffer from a great burden of unintelligibility in regard to the KJV. I did not understand every word, but I remember experiencing that as something desirable. I sensed that someday I would understand the words.

CPH: *What about the greater difficulty of a translation like the New King James Version or the English Standard Version as opposed to easy reading translations, particularly with regard to children or people new to the Bible?*

Leland Ryken: I believe that we should not immediately put an easy reading Bible into the hands of these groups. My question has always been, What good is readability if what we are reading is not what the original authors wrote? The Bible is not an easy book to read and understand. It does not carry all its meaning on the surface. As a result, a process of education is always going to be part of understanding the Bible. The danger of giving an easy reading translation to someone is that the person will never move beyond it. Also, let me ask my question again: in what other areas of life are we content with a sixth-grade level of comprehension? Finally, in my experience, children fare just fine with the NKJV and the ESV. The difficulties have been greatly exaggerated. The latterly named translations are also much easier to memorize.

CPH: *How is a literal translation more faithful to the text than dynamic equivalent translations?*

Leland Ryken: An essentially literal translation allows us to see what the biblical authors actually wrote. Much of the time dynamic equivalent translations substitute something in place of what the authors wrote. The prefaces to these translations are often quite explicit that the translators felt no obligation to give an English equivalent of what the biblical authors wrote. I personally experience dynamic equivalent translations as an organized conspiracy to prevent readers from knowing what the biblical authors wrote. As the years roll by, dynamic equivalent translations remove the Bible reading public farther and farther from the actual text of the Bible.

CPH: *How does a dynamic equivalent translation deprive readers of the full interpretive potential of the original text?*

Leland Ryken: Dynamic equivalent translations regularly make preemptive interpretive strikes, thereby removing the reader's ability to know what the original authors wrote and what the interpretive options are. Additionally, the more literary a text is, the more likely it is to embody multiple meanings in a given detail in the text. Dynamic equivalent translators regularly reduce the multiple meanings to one by the way they translate a passage. Dynamic equivalent translations are one-dimensional in places where the original is multi-dimensional. Dynamic equivalent translators are like the priests in the Middle Ages: they dole out to the public their preferred interpretation of the biblical text in a misguided effort to protect the public from what they think are incorrect interpretations.

CPH: *How are most dynamic equivalent translations like a commentary rather than a translation?*

Leland Ryken: They are like a commentary because they have an abundance of exposition or explanation mingled right in the text. Sometimes this commentary takes the form of a substitution (for example, "my feet had nearly slipped" is translated as "my faith was almost gone"). The other practice is to add an explanation to what the biblical authors wrote, as when the original says "my cup overflows" and a translation adds "my cup overflows with blessings."

CPH: *Do you see any usefulness in dynamic equivalent translations?*

Leland Ryken: I do, but not as a translation of the original text. I cannot trust dynamic equivalent translations to tell me what the biblical authors wrote. I can use them as commentaries. They give me a menu of options concerning the possible meanings of a biblical passage. However, note that I said "menu of options." Dynamic equivalent translations are less helpful than regular commentaries because they give such a wide range of renditions of many passages. They are all over the board. Therefore, I occasionally consult a few dynamic equivalent translations when I find a difficult passage, but I am more inclined to consult the footnotes in a good study Bible.

CPH: *At what point does a translation become too literal?*

Leland Ryken: A translation needs to make sense in English. If the original text contains idiomatic constructions that had an understood meaning in the original context but that make no sense in English, of course, translators need to "go dynamic." But essentially literal translators do this only in extreme situations—situations that are so few that they are perhaps statistically insignificant. Essentially literal translators regard most idiomatic constructions as figurative or poetic statements that need to be preserved, not as foreign idioms that need to be eliminated. I will just add in passing that dynamic equivalent translators have a uniformly low view of poetry and figurative language.

CPH: *Which translation do you regard as most trustworthy and excellent?*

Leland Ryken: I am a member of the translation committee of the English Standard Version, and I highly prefer it. It has a double superiority over other translations. First, it is accurate because it gives an equivalent English word or phrase for everything that biblical authors wrote. At this level of accuracy, I have equal confidence in the New American Standard Bible and the New King James Version. But the ESV has a stylistic superiority over those two translations. The ESV retains the stylistic excellence of the King James Version and flows beautifully.

CHAPTER 5 Basics of Bible Translation

This is a short introduction to the basics of Bible translation, with later chapters readdressing some areas herein, in greater detail.

John Wycliffe (1330?-84), was a Catholic priest and renowned Oxford theologian. He is credited with producing the first complete English Bible. Of course, this was a handwritten edition and produced from the Latin Vulgate and not the original language of Hebrew and Greek. It is William Tyndale (1494–1536), who produced the first printed edition of the New Testament from the original languages of Hebrew and Greek. Our modern English translations begin with the 1901 American Standard Version.

Those who wish to read the Bible, likely only have access to translations, as it was originally written in ancient Hebrew, some Aramaic, and Greek. As of 2010, there are 6,900 languages spoken in the world today, with 2,100 still needing the Bible translated into their language. (Wycliffe Translators)[1] The English-speaking world has over 100 different translations while others have just one. In fact, the Bible has even been translated into Klingon, the made-up language of the television show Star Trek. If we are one of the fortunate ones who have a choice, we certainly want to choose the Bible that is literal, accurate, clear, natural, and easy-to-understand.

The question that begs to be asked is, 'why the need for so many English translations?' There are several reasons, but as is true with many things in life, it can be taken to the extreme. The primary reason is that the English language changes over time. We no longer speak

---

[1] http://www.wycliffe.org/About/Statistics.aspx

the way of the King James Version or the American Standard Version. Another reason is that other methods of translating have come on the scene in the 1950s, which has caused a plethora of new translations: the easy-to-read dynamic equivalents and the paraphrases. Another basic reason is that even literal translation will differ in minute ways is because of textual, literary and grammatical problems that translators must make choices over.

The Words and Their Meaning

After the translation committee has established, which critical [master] text they are going to work from, they must still work the evidence of each word that has significant variants. Once it has been determined what the original language word is, its meaning must be established. The Hebrew Old Testament has hundreds of words that have not been found outside of the Old Testament itself. Let us look at an example.

1 Samuel 13:21 King James Version (KJV)

[21]Yet they had a file [Heb., *pim*] for the mattocks, and for the coulters, and for the forks, and for the axes, and to sharpen the goads.

What was a pim? It would not be uncovered until 1907 when archaeology discovered the first pim weight stone at the ancient city of Gezer. The translation, like the above King James Version, struggled in their translation of the word "pim." Today, translators know that the pim was a weight measure of about 7.82 grams, or as the English Standard Version has it, "two-thirds of a shekel," a common Hebrew unit of weight that the Philistines charged for sharpening the Israelites plowshares and mattocks.

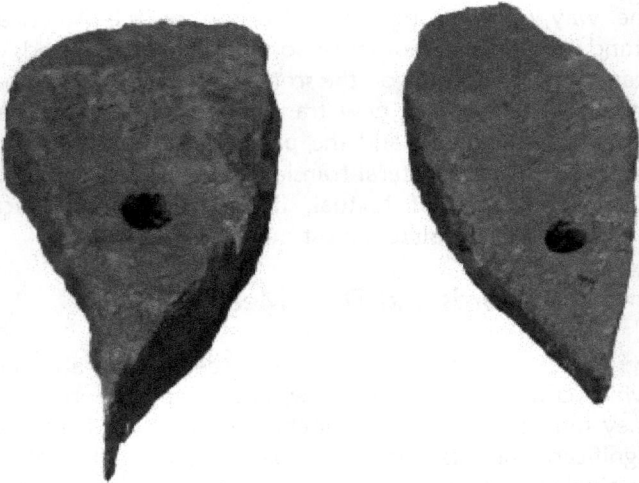

Weight inscribed with the word pym Z.
Radovan/www.BibleLandPictures.com[2]

1 Samuel 13:21 Updated American Standard Version (UASV)

[21] The charge was a pim [Heb. *pim*] for the plowshares and for the mattocks, for the three-pronged fork, for the axes, and for fixing the oxgoad.

The Greek New Testament does not face the same challenges, as there are a mere handful of words that does not appear outside of the New Testament literature. We can look at one example though from Jesus' model prayer.

Matthew 6:11 Updated American Standard Version (UASV)

[11] Give us this day our daily [Gr., *epiousion*] bread,

---

[2] http://biblia.com/books/zibbcot02/1Sa14.1-14

Here, "*epiousion*" is defined in the lexicon as either "daily" bread or "bread for tomorrow."[3] The policy of almost all modern translations is to use both words if a given Hebrew or Greek word can be taken in two different ways. Generally, they select one for the translation; the other will be placed in a footnote as "or."

The Punctuation in Translation

For centuries, there was no punctuation in the earliest Greek manuscripts of the Bible. Punctuation marks started to be introduced by copyist and translators, in accordance with their interpretation of context, as well as their understanding of Bible doctrine. There is one verse, which captures the seriousness of the modern translator, making the choice of punctuation, i.e., Luke 23:43. Depending on where the translation places the comma, you have a completely different outcome.

(1) Jesus answered him, "Truly I tell you, today you will be with me in paradise." Alternatively,

(2) Jesus answered him, "Truly I tell you today; you will be with me in paradise."

With number **(1)**, you have Jesus telling the criminal that sided with him eventually, "today you will be with me in paradise." With number **(2)**, you have Jesus telling the criminal today, "you will be with me in paradise." In other words, number **(2)** tells us that the criminal was being told this day, the day he and Jesus were speaking, that he would be with Jesus in paradise. This would mean that the criminal would die with the guarantee of an immediate future resurrection. Moreover, if the criminal were resurrected that day, it would conflict with the fact

---

[3] William Arndt, Frederick W. Danker and Walter Bauer, *A Greek-English Lexicon of the New Testament and Other Early Christian Literature*, 3rd ed. (Chicago: University of Chicago Press, 2000), 376.

Jesus was not resurrected that day. Jesus remained in the tomb for parts of three days.

The Grammar in Translation

The grammar of Hebrew and Greek can present multiple problems. The initial problem is which words should be transliterated. The Hebrew word 'adam' means "Adam" or "man." When should it be translated "Adam," and when should it be translated "man."

Genesis 1:26 Updated American Standard Version (UASV)

²⁶ And God went on to say, "Let us make man ['*adam*] in our image, after our likeness.

Genesis 3:17 Updated American Standard Version (UASV)

¹⁷ And to Adam ['*adam*] he said,

By looking at both the ancient translations, as well as the modern ones, we see a major disagreement. At Genesis 2:7 the Targum Pseudo-Jonathan uses "Adam." The Greek Septuagint does not use Adam until 2:16; and the Latin Vulgate, at 2:19. Moving to modern translations, we find the New American Standard Bible at 2:20, the New International Version at 2:21; the New English Bible at 3:21; and the New Revised Standard Version at 5:1. Other difficult choices are with the Greek word Christos, which means "Christ," or "anointed one." Additionally, Should the Greek verb *baptizo*, be transliterated as "baptize," or translated as "immerse?" Moreover, should the Hebrew word *sheol* and the Greek word *hades* be transliterated, as it is confusing when it is translated as "hell," as "death," "grave," as well as other renderings? Should Gehenna, Tartarus, and others be transliterated as opposed to translating them?

Another translation issue of late is the gender-inclusive issue. The question before a translation committee is whether the masculine-oriented Bible should stay that way. What these gender-inclusive translators fail to understand is this: to deviate, in any way, from the pattern, or likeness of how God brought his Word into existence, merely opens the Bible up to a book that reflects the age and time of its readers. If we allow the Bible to be altered because the progressive woman's movement feels offended by masculine language, it will not be long before the Bible gives way to the homosexual communities being offended by God's Words in the book of Romans; so modern translations will then tame that language, so as to not cause offense. I am certain that we thought that we would never see the day of two men, or two women being married by priests, but that day has been upon us for some time now. In fact, the American government is debating whether to change the definition of marriage. Therefore, it is suggested that the liberal readers not take the warning here as radicalism, but more like reality.

The Most Important Choice

The most important decision a Christian can make is, 'which translation should be my study Bible?' If we are to make an informed choice on which translation, is best, we need to consider the following questions: What are the different types of translations available to us, and how is each to be best used? Of the different types, what are the strong points and weaknesses? Thus, if there are weaknesses, why should you be cautious? For the purpose of this chapter, we are only considering the English language translation. In addition, while we could demonstrate with both Hebrew and Greek, to keep it simple we will only use Greek in the examples. In addition, we will use the actual Greek font, but this will not affect those who do not know Greek. The different types of translations cover a wide-range of styles, but there are three basic categories.

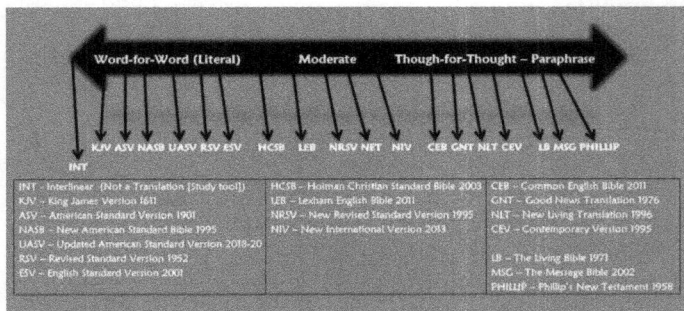

One can look at these three different styles of translations as different stages in the Bible translation process. The interlinear stage is not a Bible translation. The interlinear stage is a very rough stage of sorts, in that it does not have a smooth, clear, natural, flow, nor is it in an easy-to-understand format. However, the interlinear is a tool, and not meant to be smooth as you will see below. The literal translation is a much smoother and clearer translation when compared with an interlinear, and should be our choice of a study Bible. The dynamic equivalent is much smoother and easy-to-read, with the paraphrase being very conversational-informal (every day). However, one has to ask, at what point are we moving beyond the **Word** of God, and into a smooth, clear, easy-to-understand translation, that has hidden or obscured the original language text.

The interlinear Study Tool: This study tool could be known as a hyper-literal translation. The interlinear follows the original language **without any concern** for English grammar and syntax. Beneath the Hebrew or Greek words of the original language text, depending upon which testament you are working with, the lexical English equivalent is placed. The Greek New Testament, 2004 (UBS[4]); The Nestle-Aland Greek New Testament, 2004 (NA[27]); The Lexham Greek-English Interlinear New

Testament, 2008-2010 (LGNTI); The Lexham Hebrew-English Interlinear Old Testament, 2004 (LHB).

The Literal Translation: The literal translation is commonly called the word-for-word translation. Unlike the interlinear, the literal translation follows the original language **with concern** for English grammar and syntax. The literal translation seeks to render the original language words and style into a corresponding English word and style. Again, they seek to retain the original syntax and sentence structure, and the style of each Bible writer **as far as possible**. For example, we have the King James Version, 1611 (KJV); American Standard Version, 1901 (ASV); Revised Standard Version, 1952 (RSV); New American Standard Bible, 1995 (NASB); English Standard Version, 2001 (ESV); and the Updated American Standard Version, 2018 (UASV).

Dynamic Equivalent Dishonesty

There has become a pattern for those who favor a dynamic equivalent translation, to use an interlinear Bible, which is not a translation, and refers to it as a word for word translation, because they know that this phrase is tied to translations like the KJV, ASV, RSV, ESV, and NASB. Below is an example from Duvall and Hays in the third edition of Grasping God's Word (GGW).

Grasping God's Word by J. Scott Duvall and Daniel J. Hays is a great book, so please take what is said with a grain of salt. However, what is quoted below is very dishonest, wrong, misleading, and shows the length one will go to, to biasedly express their preference in translation philosophy. Within the table below are the egregious words from GGW.

Approaches to Translating God's Word
The process of translating is more complicated than it appears. Some people think that all you have to do

when making a translation is to define each word and string together all the individual word meanings. This assumes that the source language (in this case, Greek or Hebrew) and the receptor language (such as English) are exactly alike. If life could only be so easy! In fact, no two languages are exactly alike. For example, look at a verse chosen at random–from the story of Jesus healing a demon-possessed boy (Matt. 17:18). The word-for-word English rendition is written below a transliteration of the Greek:

Kai epetimēsen autō ho Iēsous kai exēlthen ap' autou to daimonior

And rebuked it the Jesus and came out from him the demon

kai etherapeuthē ho pais apo tēs hōras ekeinēs

and was healed the boy from the hour that

Should we conclude that the English line is the most accurate translation of Matthew 17:18 because it attempts a literal rendering of the verse, keeping also the word order? Is a translation better if it tries to match each word in the source language with a corresponding word in a receptor language? Could you even read an entire Bible "translated" in this way?[4]

Because these authors favor the dynamic equivalent translation philosophy, they misrepresent the literal translation philosophy here, to the extent of dishonesty. They give you, the reader, an interlinear rendering of Matthew 17:18, and then refer or infer that it is a literal translation, which by association would include the ASV, RSV, NASB, ESV, and the UASV. Again, an interlinear is not a Bible translation; it is a Bible study tool for persons who do not read Hebrew or Greek. What is placed under the Greek is the lexical rendering, while not considering

---

[4] Duvall, J. Scott; Hays, J. Daniel (2012-05-01). *Grasping God's Word: A Hands-On Approach to Reading, Interpreting, and Applying the Bible* (Kindle Locations 494-507). Zondervan. Kindle Edition.

grammar and syntax, i.e., they are the words in isolation. Now, to demonstrate that J. Scott Duvall and Daniel J. Hays are being disingenuous at best, let us look at the literal translations, to see if they read anything like the interlinear that Duvall and Hays used; or rather, do the literal translations consider grammar and syntax when they bring the Greek over into their English translation.

ASV	NASB	UASV
[18] And Jesus rebuked him; and the demon went out of him: and the boy was cured from that hour.	[18] And Jesus rebuked him, and the demon came out of him, and the boy was cured at once.	[18] And Jesus rebuked him, and the demon came out of him and the boy was healed from that hour.
RSV	**ESV**	**CSB**
[18] And Jesus rebuked him, and the demon came out of him, and the boy was cured instantly.	[18] And Jesus rebuked the demon, and it came out of him, and the boy was healed instantly.	[18] Then Jesus rebuked the demon, and it came out of him, and from that moment the boy was healed.

As can be clearly seen from the above four literal translations (ASV, NASB, UASV, and the RSV) and the essentially literal ESV and the optimally literal CSB, they are nothing like the interlinear that Duvall and Hays tried to pawn off on us as a word-for-word translation, i.e., a literal translation. The reader can decide for himself if this is misleading or dishonest.

The Dynamic or Functional Equivalent: This is actually going beyond the Word of God. This method of translation is fine for those few verses that would be misunderstood or even meaningless if it were left literal. For example, 1 Peter 3:3 reads, "Do not let your adorning [*kosmos*, literally "world"] be external, the braiding of hair and the putting on of gold jewelry, or the clothing you wear." It would be nonsensical if it were left literally to read, "Do not let your **world** be external, the braiding of hair and the putting on of gold jewelry, or the clothing you wear."

The DE or thought-for-thought translation philosophy (dynamic equivalent) seeks to render the biblical meaning of the original language text as accurately as possible into an English informal (conversational) equivalent. For example, to mention just a few, we have Today's English Version, 1976 (TEV, GNB); Contemporary English Version, 1995 (CEV); New Living Translation (second edition), 2004 (NLT).

Paraphrase translations are the furthest removed from the interlinear stage. The translators of these Bibles, if we dare to call them such, render the original language into the target language as freely as they feel it needs to be, with the target audience being their most important concern. For example, we have The Living Bible, 1971 (TLB) and The Message Bible, 2002 (MSG).

The Moderate Translation: Like anything in life, there is a tendency to strike a balance between two polarizing worlds, such as the literal translation and the dynamic equivalent. These versions of the Bible endeavor to express the words as well as the meaning and essence of the original-language expressions while also making the text easier to read. For example, we have the New English Translation, 1996 (NET); Holman Christian Standard Bible, 2003 (HCSB); and the New International Version, 2011 (NIV). However, this gesture is a slippery slope for two reasons (1) there is no need to drop below a literal translation level, to do so is to dilute the Word of God. (2) In addition, a step toward the dynamic equivalent is usually followed by another step before long. For example, the 1984 New International Version was an attempt at the middle ground, but the 2011 edition of the NIV went another step toward the dynamic equivalent camp.

CHAPTER 6 Translation Philosophy

The debate as to where one should be in the spectrum of literal versus dynamic equivalent, i.e., their translation philosophy has been going on since the first translation of the Hebrew (Aramaic) into Greek, i.e., the Septuagint (280-150 B.C.E.). However, if we were to look to the first printed English translation of 1526 by William Tyndale, we would find a literal translation philosophy that ran for almost four-hundred-years. It was not until the 20th century that we find the wholesale overthrow of the literal translation philosophy. For every literal English translation that we have today, there are dozens of dynamic equivalent translations. Just to name a few, we have the Contemporary Version, the Good News Translation, the Easy to Read Version, the New Life Version, the New Living Translation, God's Word, the New Century Version, the New International Reader's Version, and the like. Below, we will offer a deeper discussion of these translation philosophies than we had in the previous chapter, which had simply served as an introduction to the subject.

Interlinear Study Tool

The interlinear Bible page is set up with the left column where you will find the original language text, with the English word-for-word lexical gloss beneath each original language word; generally, the right column contains an English translation like the ESV, NASB, or the NIV. The interlinear translation in the left column and the modern-day English translation in the right column are parallel to each other. This allows the student to make immediate comparisons between the translation and the interlinear, helping one to determine the accuracy of the translation.

καὶ λέγει αὐτῇ ὁ Ἰησοῦς, Τί ἐμοὶ καὶ σοί, γύναι;
And says to her the Jesus what to me and to you woman

οὔπω ἥκει ἡ ὥρα μου.
Not yet is come the hour of me

THE GOSPEL ACCORDING TO
MATTHEW

KATA MAΘΘAION
ACCORDING TO MATTHEW

1.1 Βίβλος γενέσεως Ἰησοῦ Χριστοῦ υἱοῦ Δαυὶδ
A RECORD OF [THE] GENEALOGY OF JESUS CHRIST SON OF DAVID

υἱοῦ Ἀβραάμ.
SON OF ABRAHAM.

1.2 Ἀβραὰμ ἐγέννησεν τὸν Ἰσαάκ, Ἰσαὰκ δὲ
ABRAHAM FATHERED ISAAC, AND-ISAAC

ἐγέννησεν τὸν Ἰακώβ, Ἰακὼβ δὲ ἐγέννησεν τὸν Ἰούδαν
FATHERED JACOB. AND-JACOB FATHERED JUDAH

καὶ τοὺς ἀδελφοὺς αὐτοῦ, **1.3** Ἰούδας δὲ ἐγέννησεν τὸν
AND THE BROTHERS OF HIM, AND-JUDAH FATHERED

Φάρες καὶ τὸν Ζάρα ἐκ τῆς Θαμάρ, Φάρες δὲ
PEREZ AND ZERAH BY TAMAR, AND-PEREZ

ἐγέννησεν τὸν Ἑσρώμ, Ἑσρὼμ δὲ ἐγέννησεν τὸν
FATHERED HEZRON, AND-HEZRON FATHERED

Ἀράμ, **1.4** Ἀρὰμ δὲ ἐγέννησεν τὸν Ἀμιναδάβ,
ARAM, AND-ARAM FATHERED AMMINADAB.

Ἀμιναδὰβ δὲ ἐγέννησεν τὸν Ναασσών, Ναασσὼν δὲ
AND-AMMINADAB FATHERED NASHON, AND-NASHON

ἐγέννησεν τὸν Σαλμών, **1.5** Σαλμὼν δὲ ἐγέννησεν τὸν
FATHERED SALMON, AND-SALMON FATHERED

Βόες ἐκ τῆς Ῥαχάβ, Βόες δὲ ἐγέννησεν τὸν Ἰωβὴδ ἐκ
BOAZ BY RAHAB, AND-BOAZ FATHERED OBED BY

τῆς Ῥούθ, Ἰωβὴδ δὲ ἐγέννησεν τὸν Ἰεσσαί,
RUTH, AND-OBED FATHERED JESSE.

1.6 Ἰεσσαὶ δὲ ἐγέννησεν τὸν Δαυὶδ τὸν βασιλέα.
AND-JESSE FATHERED DAVID THE KING.

Δαυὶδ δὲ ἐγέννησεν τὸν Σολομῶνα ἐκ τῆς τοῦ
AND-DAVID FATHERED SOLOMON BY THE [WIFE]

An account of the genealogy[a] of Jesus the Messiah,[b] the son of David, the son of Abraham.

2 Abraham was the father of Isaac, and Isaac the father of Jacob, and Jacob the father of Judah and his brothers, ³and Judah the father of Perez and Zerah by Tamar, and Perez the father of Hezron, and Hezron the father of Aram, ⁴and Aram the father of Aminadab, and Aminadab the father of Nahshon, and Nahshon the father of Salmon, ⁵and Salmon the father of Boaz by Rahab, and Boaz the father of Obed by Ruth, and Obed the father of Jesse, ⁶and Jesse the father of King David.

And David was the father of Solomon by the wife of Uriah, ⁷and Solomon the father of Rehoboam, and Rehoboam the father of Abijah, and Abijah the father of Asaph,[c] ⁸and Asaph the father of Jehoshaphat, and Jehoshaphat the father of Joram, and Joram the father of Uzziah, ⁹and Uzziah the father of

[a] *Or* birth
[b] *Or* Jesus Christ
[c] Other ancient authorities read Asa

The New Greek-English Interlinear NT by Tyndale Publishing

The interlinear and the English equivalent in the left column are not generated by taking the English word(s) from the translation on the right and then placing them under the original language text. Whether we are dealing with Hebrew or Greek as our original language text, each word will have two or more English equivalents. What factors go into the choice of which word will go under the original language word? One factor is the period in which the book was written. As the New Testament was penned in the first century, during the era of Koine Greek, as opposed to classical Greek of centuries past, and then there is the context of what comes before and after the word under consideration.

Therefore, the translator will use his training in the original language, or a lexicon to determine if he is working with a noun, verb, the definite article, adjective, adverb, preposition, conjunction, participle, and the like. Further, say he is looking at the verb, it must be determined what mood it is in (indicative, subjunctive, imperative, etc.), what tense (present, future, aorist, etc.), what voice (active, middle, passive, etc.), and so forth. In addition, the English words under the original language text are generated from grammatical form, the alterations to the root, which affect its role within the sentence, for which he will look to the Hebrew or Greek grammar reference.

The best lexicon is the 3rd edition Greek-English Lexicon of the New Testament and other Early Christian Literature, (BDAG) ten years in the making, this extensive revision of Bauer, the standard authority worldwde, features new entries, 15,000 additional references from ancient literature, clearer type, and extended definitions rather than one-word synonyms. Providing a more panoramic view of the world and language of the New Testament, it becomes the new indispensable guide for translators. The second-best lexicon is the Greek-English Lexicon: With a Revised Supplement, 1996: Ninth Revsed Edition - Edited By H.G. Liddell, R. Scott by H.G. Liddell & R. Scott. Each word is given in root form along with important variations, and an excellent representation of examples from classical, Koine and Attic Greek sources follows. This lexicon is appropriate for all classical Greek and general biblical studies. By far the best traditional Hebrew lexicon currently available is The Hebrew and Aramaic Lexicon of the Old Testament (HALOT) (vols. 1-5; trans. M. E. J. Richardson; Brill, 1994-2000). However, the price is beyond most students and scholars. A more affordable edition, which I highly recommend, is available, Hebrew and Aramaic Lexicon of the Old Testament (Unabridged 2-Volume Study Edition) (2 vols. trans. M. E. J. Richardson; Brill, 2002).

There are numerous lexicons on the market, which would be fine tools for the Bible student. Many scholars would concur that Biblical lexicons have four main weaknesses:

(1) They are geared toward the translations of the 20th century, as opposed to new translations.

(2) They primarily contain only information from the Bible itself, as opposed to possessing information from Greek literature overall.

(3) They are too narrow as to the words of say the New Testament, attempting to harmonize a word and its meaning. The problem with this agenda is that a word can have numerous meanings, some being quite different, depending on its context, even by the same author.

(4) Most Biblical lexicons have not escaped the etymological fallacy, determining the meaning of a word based on its origin and past meaning(s). Another aspect being that the meaning of a word is based on the internal structure of the word. A common English example of the latter is "butterfly." The separate part of "butter" and "fly" do not define "butterfly." Another example is "ladybird."

7 μὴ θαυμάσῃς ὅτι εἶπόν σοι,   Δεῖ
Not marvel   that I said to you it is necessary

ὑμᾶς γεννηθῆναι ἄνωθεν
you to be born   from above

5

⁷ Do not marvel that I said to you, 'It is necessary for you to be born again.'[6]

As you can see the interlinear translation reads very rough, as it is following the Greek sentence structure. The Updated American Standard Version rearranges the words according to English grammar and syntax. Do not be surprised that at times words may need to be left out of the English translation, as they are unnecessary.   For example, The Greek language sometimes likes to put the definite article "the" before personal name, so in the Greek, you may have "the Jesus said." In the English, it would be appropriate to drop the definite article. At other times, it may be appropriate to add words to complete the sense in the English translation. For example, at John 4:26, Jesus said to the Samaritan woman, "I, the one speaking to you, am he." *The word "he" is not in the Greek text but is implied, so it is added to complete the sense. Please see the image on the next page.

---

⁵ Kurt Aland et al., *The Greek New Testament, Fourth Revised Edition (Interlinear with Morphology)* (Deutsche Bibelgesellschaft, 1993; 2006), Jn 3:7.

⁶ Edward Andrews et al., *The Updated American Standard Version* (Christian Publishing House, 2014; 2018), Jn 3:7.

26λέγει αὐτῇ ὁ Ἰησοῦς, Ἐγώ εἰμι, ὁ λαλῶν σοι
Says to her the Jesus I am the one speaking to you

Literal: I am the one speaking to you
ESV: "I who speak to you am he."

The Greek New Testament, (Interlinear)

Here in John chapter 4, you have Jesus being spoken to by a Samaritan woman. She is inquiring about the coming Messiah, and Jesus does something with the Samaritan woman that he has not done even with his disciples, He discloses who he really is, "I am the one [i.e., the Messiah]. The ESV, like the other translations that we have considered, is aware that there is an implied predicate pronoun in the sentence "I am [he] the one speaking to you."

Literal Translation

Once the interlinear level has taken place, it is now time to adjust our English lexical glosses into sentences. Each word will possess its own grammatical indicator. As the translator begins to construct his English sentence, he will adjust according to the context of the words surrounding his focus. As you will see shortly, in the examples below, the translator must transition the words from the Greek order, to correct English grammar and syntax. This is a delicate balance faced by the literal translation team. As they must determine how close they will cling to the Hebrew or Greek word order in their English translation. The reader will find that the KJV, ASV, NASB, ESV and the UASV will allow a little roughness for the reader, for them an acceptable sacrifice as they believe that meaning is conveyed by the word order at times. An overly simplified example might be Christ Jesus as opposed to Jesus Christ, with the former focusing on the office ("Christ" anointed one), while the latter focuses on the person.

Even though it is impossible to follow the word order of the original in an English translation, the translator will attempt to stay as close as possible to the effective and persuasive use that the style of the original language permits. In other words, what is stated in the original language is rendered into the English, as well as the way that it is said, as far as possible? This is why the literal translation is known as a "formal equivalence." As a literal translation, it "is designed so as to reveal as much of the original form as possible. (Ray 1982, p. 47)

It should be noted that this writer favors the literal translation over the dynamic equivalent, and especially the paraphrase. The literal translation gives us what God said; there is no concealing this by going beyond into the realms of what a translator interprets these words as saying. It should be understood that God's Word to man is not meant to be read like a John Grisham novel. It is meant to be meditated on, pondered over, and absorbed quite slowly; using many tools and helps along the way. There is a reason for this, it is that the Bible is a sifter of hearts. It separates out those who really want to know and understand God's Word (based on their evident demonstration of buying out the opportune time for study and research), from those who have no real motivation, no interest, just going through life. Even though, literal translation method needs to be done in a balanced manner, and should not be taken too far.

There are times when a literal word-for-word translation is **not** in the best interest of the reader and could convey a meaning contrary to the original.

(1) As we have established throughout this book, but have not stated directly, no two languages are exactly equivalent in grammar, vocabulary, and sentence structure.

Ephesians 4:14 Updated American Standard Version (UASV

¹⁴ So that we may no longer be children, tossed to and fro by the waves and carried about by every wind of teaching, by the trickery [lit., dice playing] of men, by craftiness with regard to the scheming of deceit;

The Greek word *kybeia* that is usually rendered "craftiness" or "trickery," is literally "dice-playing," which refers to the practice of cheating others when playing dice. If it was rendered literally, "carried about by every wind of doctrine, by the trickery dice-playing of men," the meaning would be lost. Therefore, the meaning of what the original author meant by his use of the Greek word *kybeia*, must be the translator's choice.

Romans 12:11 Updated American Standard Version (UASV)

¹¹ Do not be slothful in zeal,⁷ be fervent in spirit, serving the Lord;

When Paul wrote the Romans, he used the Greek word *zeontes*, which literally means, "boil," "seethe," or "fiery hot." Some serious Bible students may notice the thought of "boiling in spirit," as being "fervent in spirit or better "aglow with the spirit," or "keep your spiritual fervor." Therefore, for the sake of making sense, it is best to take the literal "boiling in spirit," determine what is meant by the author's use of the Greek word *zeontes*, "keep your spiritual fervor", and render it thus.

Matthew 5:3 New International Version, ©2011 (NIV)

³ "Blessed are the poor in spirit, for theirs is the kingdom of heaven.

---

⁷ Or *diligent*

Matthew 5:3 GOD'S WORD Translation (GW)

³"Blessed are those who [are poor in spirit] recognize they are spiritually helpless. The kingdom of heaven belongs to them.

This one is a tough call. The phrase "poor in spirit" carries so much history, and has been written as to what it means, for almost 2,000 years that, even the dynamic equivalent translations are unwilling to translate its meaning, not its words. Personally, this writer is in favor of the literal translation of "poor in spirit." Those who claim to be literal translators should not back away because "poor in spirit" is ambiguous, and there is a variety of interpretations. The above dynamic equivalent translation, God's Word, has come closest to what was meant. Actually, "poor" is even somewhat of an interpretation, because the Greek word *ptochos* means "beggar." Therefore, "poor in spirit" is an interpretation of "beggar in spirit." The extended interpretation is that the "beggar/poor in spirit" is aware of his or her spiritual needs as if a beggar or the poor would be aware of their physical needs.

(2) As we have also established in this chapter a word's meaning can be different, depending on the context that it was used.

2 Samuel 8:3 Updated American Standard Version (UASV)

³ Then David struck down Hadadezer, the son of Rehob king of Zobah, as he went to restore his authority **[lit. hand]** at the River.

1 Kings 10:13 Updated American Standard Version (UASV)

¹³ King Solomon gave to the queen of Sheba all her desire which she requested, besides what he gave her according to his royal bounty **[li. hand]**. Then she turned and went to her own land, she together with her servants.

Proverbs 18:21 Updated American Standard Version (UASV)

²¹ Death and life are in the power **[lit. hand]** of the tongue, and those who love it will eat its fruits.

The English word "hand" has no meaning outside of its context. It could mean, "end of the arm," "pointer on a clock," "card players," "round in a card game," "part in doing something," "round of applause," "member of a ship's crew," or "worker." The Hebrew word "*yad*," which means "hand," has many meanings as well, depending on the context, as it can mean "control," "bounty," or "power." This one word is translated in more than forty different ways in some translations. Let us look at some English sentences, to see the literal way of using "hand," and then add what it means, as a new sentence.

- Please give a big *hand* to our next contestant. Please give a big *applause* for our next contestant.
- Your future is in your own *hands*. Your future is in your own *power*. Your future is in your own *possession*.
- Attention, all *hands!* Attention, all *ship's crew!*
- She has a good *hand* for gardening. She has a good *ability* or *skill* for gardening.
- Please give me a hand; I need some help.
- The copperplate writing was beautifully written; she has a nice hand.

At times, even a literal translation committee will not render a word the same every time it occurs, because the sense is not the same every time. The only problem we have is that the reader must now be dependent on the judgment of the translator to select the right word(s) that reflect the meaning of the original language word accurately and understandably. Let us look at the above texts from the Hebrew Old Testament again, this time doing what we did with the English word "hand" in the above. It is debatable if any of these verses really needed to be more explicit, by giving the meaning in the translation, as opposed to the word itself.

2 Samuel 8:3: who went to restore his *hand* at the Euphrates River – who went to restore his control at the Euphrates River

1 Kings 10:13: she asked besides what was given her by the *hand* of King Solomon - she asked besides what was given her by the *bounty* of King Solomon

Proverbs 18:21: Death and life are in the *hand* of the tongue - Death and life are in the power of the tongue

We can look to one example translation, who touts the fact that it is a literal translation, i.e., the English Standard Version (ESV). In fact, it waters that concept down by qualifying its literalness, saying that it is an essentially literal translation. Essentially means being the most basic element or feature of something. In this case, the ESV is the most basic element or feature of a literal translation. In the course of 13 years of using the ESV, this author has discovered that it unnecessarily abandons its literal translation philosophy quite regularly. Dr. William Mounce was the head of the translation committee that produced the ESV, and he leans toward or favors the dynamic equivalent translation philosophy. He has since left the ESV committee and has become the head of the New International Version committee, which is being more and more of a dynamic equivalent, with each new edition. This is not to say that the ESV is not a splendid translation because it is.

Dynamic Equivalent Translation

Translators who produce what are frequently referred to as free translations, take liberties with the text as presented in the original languages. How so? They either insert their opinion of what the original text could mean or omit some of the information contained in the original text. Dynamic equivalent translations may be appealing because they are easy to read. However, their very freeness at times obscures or changes the meaning of the original text.

Ecclesiastes 9:8 (NLT)	Ecclesiastes 9:8 (CEV)	Ecclesiastes 9:8 (GNT)	Ecclesiastes 9:8 (NCV)
8 Wear fine clothes, with a splash of cologne!	8 Dress up, comb your hair, and look your best.	8 Always look happy and cheerful.	8 Put on nice clothes and make yourself look good.

First, the above dynamic equivalents do not even agree with each other. What does **Ecclesiastes 9:8** really say.

Ecclesiastes 9:8 (NASB)	Ecclesiastes 9:8 (ESV)	Ecclesiastes 9:8 (UASV)	Ecclesiastes 9:8 (HCSB)
8 Let your clothes be white all the time, and let not oil be lacking on your head.	8 Let your garments be always white. Let not oil be lacking on your head.	8 Let your garments be always white, and let not your head lack oil.	8 Let your clothes be white all the time, and never let oil be lacking on your head.

What does the metaphorical language of "white garments" and "oil on your head" symbolize? Does **"white garments"** mean to "wear fine clothes," "dress up," "look happy," or "put on nice clothes"? In addition, does "oil on your head" means "a splash of cologne," "comb your hair" or "make yourself look good"? Duane Garrett says, "Wearing white clothes and anointing the hair (v. 8) symbolize joy and contrast with the familiar use of sackcloth and ashes as a sign of mourning or repentance."[8] Let us also look at an exegetical commentary as well as a book on Bible backgrounds.

John Peter Lange et al., A Commentary on the Holy Scriptures: Ecclesiastes	James M. Freeman and Harold J. Chadwick, Manners & Customs of the Bible
White garments are the expression of festive joy and pure, calm feelings in the soul, comp. Rev. 3:4 f.; 7:9 ff. Koheleth could hardly have meant a literal observance of this precept, so that the conduct of Sisinnius, Novatian bishop of Constantinople, who, with reference to this passage, always went in white garments, was very properly censured by Chrysostom as Pharisaical and proud. Hengstenberg's view is arbitrary, and in other respects scarcely corresponds to the sense of the author: "White garments are here to be put on as an expression of the confident hope of the future glory of the people of God, as Spener had himself buried in a white	In any area with strong sunlight, white clothing is preferred because white reflects the sunlight and so decreases the heating effect of it. In addition, white garments in the East were symbols of purity, and so were worn on certain special occasions. The symbols and custom were adopted by the West and is reflected especially in the wedding ceremony. The oil was symbolic of joy. Together they signified purity and the joy of festive occasions.

In the Bible there are several references to white garments symbolizing purity, righteousness, or holiness. In Daniel 7:9, the clothing worn by the "Ancient of |

---

[8] Duane A. Garrett, *Proverbs, Ecclesiastes, Song of Songs*, vol. 14, The New American Commentary (Nashville: Broadman & Holman Publishers, 1993), 331.

coffin as a sign of his hope in a better future of the Church."

And let thy head lack no ointment. As in 2 Sam. 12:20; 14:2; Isa. 61:3; Amos 6:6; Prov. 27:9; Ps. 45:8, so here appears the anointing oil, which keeps the hair smooth and makes the face to shine, as a symbol of festive joy, and a contrast to a sorrowing disposition. There is no reason here for supposing fragrant spikenard (Mark 14:2), because the question is mainly about producing a good appearance by means of the ointment, comp. Ps. 133:2. Ver. 9.[9]

Days ... was as white as snow." When Jesus was transfigured, "his clothes became as white as the light" (Matthew 17:2). The angels appeared in white robes when they appeared to the soldiers guarding Jesus' tomb and when the women went to the tomb after He had risen (Matthew 28:3, Mark 16:5, Luke 24:4, and John 20:12), and also when Christ ascended into heaven (Acts 1:10). In the ages to come, the redeemed will be clothed in white (Revelation 7:13 and 19:14).[10]

We can see that the three sources interpret the metaphorical language of "white garments" and "oil on your head" as purity and joy. Would we get this by way of the four dynamic equivalents in the above? Would "Wear fine clothes, with a splash of cologne" (NLT) get us to the correct meaning? We should not replace metaphorical language because we feel it is too difficult for the reader to understand. They should buy out the time, just as this writer has done, by going to commentaries,

---

[9] John Peter Lange et al., *A Commentary on the Holy Scriptures: Ecclesiastes* (Bellingham, WA: Logos Bible Software, 2008), 126.

[10] James M. Freeman and Harold J. Chadwick, *Manners & Customs of the Bible* (North Brunswick, NJ: Bridge-Logos Publishers, 1998), 338.

word study books, and Bible background books. Let us look at one more informative Bible background book,

9:8. clothed in white. Scholars have understood the color white to symbolize purity, festivity or elevated social status. In both Egypt Story of Sinuhe) and Mesopotamia (Epic of Gilgamesh) clean or bright garments conveyed a sense of well-being. Moreover, the hot Middle-Eastern climate favors the wearing of white clothes to reflect the heat.

9.8. anointed head. Oil preserved the complexion in the hot Middle Eastern climate. Both the Egyptian *Song of the Harper* and the Mesopotamian Epic of Gilgamesh described individuals clothed in fine linen and with myrrh on their head. (Walton, Matthews and Chavalas 2000, p. 574)

As we are about to take up the subject of the paraphrase, let us consider the above Ecclesiastes 9:8 and the surrounding verses in a paraphrase.

Ecclesiastes 9:8 (The Message)

7-10 Seize life! Eat bread with gusto.
Drink wine with a robust heart.
Oh yes, God takes pleasure in your pleasure!
Dress festively every morning.
Don't skimp on colors and scarves.
Relish life with the spouse you love
Each and every day of your precarious life.
Each day is God's gift. It's all you get in exchange
For the hard work of staying alive.
Make the most of each one!
Whatever turns up, grab it and do it. And heartily!
This is your last and only chance at it,
For there's neither work to do nor thoughts to think

In the company of the dead, where you're most certainly headed.

Paraphrase Translation

A paraphrase is "a restatement of a text, passage, or work giving the meaning in another form."[11] The highest priority and characteristic is the rephrasing and simplification. Whatever has been said in the above about the dynamic equivalent can be magnified a thousand-fold herein. The best way to express the level this translation will be to go to a paraphrase and set it side-by-side with the dynamic equivalent and literal translations. Below we have done that, i.e., **Isaiah 1:1-17.** It is recommended that we read verses 1-4 in the Message Bible, then in the New Living Translation, and then in the English Standard Version. Thereafter, read verses 5-9 in the same manner, followed by verses 10-12, and 13-17. This way we will taste the flavor of each with just a small bit at a time, so you do not lose the sense of the previous one by too much reading.

Isaiah 1:1-17 The Message (MSG)	Isaiah 1:1-17 New Living Translation (NLT)	Isaiah 1:1-17 Updated American Standard Version (UASV)
[1]The vision that Isaiah son of Amoz saw regarding Judah and Jerusalem during the times of the kings of Judah: Uzziah,	[1] These are the visions that Isaiah son of Amoz saw concerning Judah and Jerusalem. He saw these visions during	1 The vision of Isaiah the son of Amoz, which he saw concerning Judah and Jerusalem in the days of Uzziah, Jotham, Ahaz, and

---

[11] Inc Merriam-Webster, *Merriam-Webster's Collegiate Dictionary.*, Eleventh ed. (Springfield, Mass.: Merriam-Webster, Inc., 2003).

Jotham, Ahaz, and Hezekiah. ²⁻⁴Heaven and earth, you're the jury.

Listen to God's case: "I had children and raised them well, and they turned on me. The ox knows who's boss, the mule knows the hand that feeds him, But not Israel. My people don't know up from down. Shame! Misguided God-dropouts, staggering under their guilt-baggage, Gang of miscreants, band of vandals— My people have walked out on me, their God, turned their backs on The

the years when Uzziah, Jotham, Ahaz, and Hezekiah were kings of Judah.

² Listen, O heavens! Pay attention, earth! This is what the LORD says: "The children I raised and cared for have rebelled against me. ³ Even an ox knows its owner, and a donkey recognizes its master's care— but Israel doesn't know its master. My people don't recognize my care for them." ⁴ Oh, what a sinful nation they are— loaded down with a

Hezekiah, kings of Judah.

The Wickedness of Judah

² Hear, O heavens, and give ear, O earth; for Jehovah has spoken: "Sons I have brought up and raised, but they have revolted against me. ³ An ox knows its owner, and the donkey its master's manger, but Israel does not know, my people do not understand."

⁴ Woe to the sinful nation, a people weighed down with error, brood of wicked men, sons who act corruptly! They have abandoned Jehovah, they

Holy of Israel,
  walked off
and never
looked back.

  5-9"Why
bother even
trying to do
anything with
you
  when you
just keep to
your
bullheaded
ways?
You keep
beating your
heads against
brick walls.
  Everything
within you
protests
against you.
From the
bottom of
your feet to
the top of
your head,
  nothing's
working right.
Wounds and
bruises and
running
sores—
  untended,
unwashed,
unbandaged.
Your country is
laid waste,

burden of guilt.
  They are evil
people,
  corrupt
children who
have rejected
the LORD.
  They have
despised the
Holy One of
Israel
  and turned
their backs on
him.

  5 Why do you
continue to
invite
punishment?
  Must you
rebel forever?
  Your head is
injured,
  and your
heart is sick.
  6 You are
battered from
head to foot—
  covered
with bruises,
welts, and
infected
wounds—
  without
any soothing
ointments or
bandages.
  7 Your country
lies in ruins,

have despised the
Holy One of
Israel,
  they have
turned their backs
on him.

  5 Where will you
be stricken again,
  as you continue
in your rebellion??
The whole head is
sick,
  and the whole
heart faint.
  6 From the sole of
the foot even to
the head,
  there is no
soundness in it,
but bruises and
sores
  and raw
wounds;
they are not
pressed out or
bound up
  or softened
with oil.

  7 Your land is
desolate;
  your cities are
burned with fire;
in your very
presence
  foreigners
devour your land;
  it is desolate, as

your cities burned down. Your land is destroyed by outsiders while you watch,
    reduced to rubble by barbarians.
Daughter Zion is deserted—
    like a tumbledown shack on a dead-end street,
Like a tarpaper shanty on the wrong side of the tracks,
    like a sinking ship abandoned by the rats.
If God-of-the-Angel-Armies hadn't left us a few survivors,
    we'd be as desolate as Sodom,
doomed just like Gomorrah.

10"Listen to my Message,
    you Sodom-

and your towns are burned.
    Foreigners plunder your fields before your eyes
    and destroy everything they see.
8 Beautiful Jerusalem stands abandoned
    like a watchman's shelter in a vineyard,
    like a lean-to in a cucumber field after the harvest,
    like a helpless city under siege.
9 If the LORD of Heaven's Armies
    had not spared a few of us,
    we would have been wiped out like Sodom,

overthrown by foreigners.
8 And the daughter of Zion is left
    like a shelter in a vineyard,
like a hut in a cucumber field,
    like a city besieged.

9 Unless Jehovah of armies
    had left us a few survivors,
we would be like Sodom,
    we would have become like Gomorrah.

10 Hear the word of Jehovah,
    you rulers of Sodom!
Give ear to the law[12] of our God,
    you people of Gomorrah!
11 "What are your many sacrifices to me?
    says Jehovah;
I have had enough of burnt offerings of rams
    and the fat of

---

12 Or *teaching* or *instruction*

schooled leaders. Receive God's revelation, you Gomorrah-schooled people.

11-12"Why this frenzy of sacrifices?" *God's* asking. "Don't you think I've had my fill of burnt sacrifices, rams and plump grain-fed calves? Don't you think I've had my fill of blood from bulls, lambs, and goats? When you come before me, whoever gave you the idea of acting like this, Running here and there, destroyed like Gomorrah.

¹⁰ Listen to the LORD, you leaders of "Sodom." Listen to the law of our God, people of "Gomorrah."

¹¹ "What makes you think I want all your sacrifices?" says the LORD. "I am sick of your burnt offerings of rams and the fat of fattened cattle. I get no pleasure from the blood of bulls and lambs and goats.

¹² When you come to worship me, who asked you to parade well-fed animals; I do not delight in the blood of bulls, or of lambs, or of goats.

¹² "When you come to appear before me, who has required of you, this trampling of my courts?

¹³ Bring no more vain offerings; incense is an abomination to me. New moon and Sabbath and the calling of assemblies — I cannot endure iniquity¹³ and solemn assembly.

¹⁴ Your new moons and your appointed feasts my soul hates; they have become a burden to me; I am weary of bearing them.

¹⁵ When you spread out

---

¹³ Isaiah's use of (ʾāwen) may designate magic or idolatrous ritual, or evil caused by the misue of power.

doing this and that—
all this sheer commotion in the place provided for worship?

13-17"Quit your worship charades.
I can't stand your trivial religious games:
Monthly conferences, weekly Sabbaths, special meetings—
meetings, meetings, meetings—I can't stand one more!
Meetings for this, meetings for that. I hate them!
You've worn me out!
I'm sick of your religion, religion, religion,
while you go through my courts with all your ceremony?
¹³ Stop bringing me your meaningless gifts;
the incense of your offerings disgusts me!
As for your celebrations of the new moon and the Sabbath
and your special days for fasting—
they are all sinful and false.
I want no more of your pious meetings.
¹⁴ I hate your new moon celebrations and your annual festivals.
They are a burden to me. I cannot stand them!
¹⁵ When you your hands,
I will hide my eyes from you;
yes, even though you make many prayers,
I will not listen.
Your hands are full¹⁴ of blood.
¹⁶ Wash yourselves; make yourselves clean;
remove the evil of your deeds from before my eyes;
cease to do evil,
¹⁷ learn to do good;
seek justice,
correct the oppresor;
bring justice to the fatherless,
plead for the widow.

---

¹⁴ Or *covered with*

right on sinning. When you put on your next prayer-performance, I'll be looking the other way. No matter how long or loud or often you pray, I'll not be listening. And do you know why? Because you've been tearing people to pieces, and your hands are bloody. Go home and wash up. Clean up your act. Sweep your lives clean of your evildoings so I don't have to look at them any longer. Say no to wrong. Learn to do good. Work for

lift up your hands in prayer, I will not look.
    Though you offer many prayers, I will not listen,
    for your hands are covered with the blood of innocent victims.
[16] Wash yourselves and be clean!
    Get your sins out of my sight.
    Give up your evil ways.
[17] Learn to do good.
    Seek justice.
  Help the oppressed.
    Defend the cause of orphans.
    Fight for the rights of widows.

| justice.
    Help   the
down-and-out.
Stand   up   for
the   homeless.
    Go to bat for
the defenseless. | | |

Literal Contrasted with Dynamic Equivalent

In short, the dynamic equivalent translator seeks to render the biblical meaning of the original language text as accurately as possible into an English informal (conversational) equivalent. Alternatively, the literal translation seeks to render the original language words and style into a corresponding English word and style.

Again, there are two major divisions in translation philosophy. We have the word-for-word and the thought-for-thought. A literal translation is one-step removed from the original, and something is always lost or gained, because there will never be 100 percent equivalent transference from one language to the next. A thought-for-thought translation is one more step removed than the literal translation in many cases and can block the sense of the original entirely. A thought-for-thought translation slants the text in a particular direction, cutting off other options and nuances.

A literal word-for-word translation makes every effort to represent the authority, power, vitality and directness of the original Hebrew and Greek Scriptures accurately and to transfer these characteristics in modern English. The literal translations have the goal of producing as literal a translation as possible where the modern-English idiom permits and where a literal rendering does not conceal the thought. Again, there are times when the literal rendering would be unintelligible, and so one must interpret what the author meant by the words that he used.

Literal Translation	Dynamic Equivalent
Focuses on form	Focuses on meaning
Emphasizes source language	Emphasizes receptor language
Translates what was said	Translates what was meant
Presumes original context	Presumes contemporary context
Retains ambiguities	Removes ambiguities
Minimizes interpretative bias	Enhances interpretative bias
Valuable for serious Bible study	Valuable for commentary use
Awkward receptor language style	Natural receptor language style

The alteration of one word can remove an enormous amount of meaning from the Word of God. Let us consider 1 Kings 2:10 as an example.

Literal Translation	Dynamic Equivalent
1 Kings 2:10 (ESV) [10] Then David **slept** with his fathers and was buried in the city of David.	1 Kings 2:10 (GNT) [10] David **died** and was buried in David's City.

1 Kings 2:10 (ASV)	1 Kings 2:10 (NLT)
[10] And David **slept** with his fathers, and was buried in the city of David.	[10] Then David **died** and was buried with his ancestors in the City of David.
1 Kings 2:10 (NASB)	**1 Kings 2:10 (GW)**
[10] Then David slept with his fathers and was buried in the city of David.	[10] David **lay down in death** with his ancestors and was buried in the City of David.
1 Kings 2:10 (UASV)	**1 Kings 2:10 (NIRV)**
[10] Then David **slept** with his fathers and was buried in the city of David.	[10] David joined the members of his family who had already **died**. His body was buried in the City of David.
1 Kings 2:10 (RSV)	**1 Kings 2:10 (NCV)**
[10] Then David **slept** with his fathers, and was buried in the city of David.	[10] Then David **died** and was buried with his ancestors in Jerusalem.

One could conclude that the (dynamic equivalent) thought-for-thought translations are conveying the idea in a more clear and immediate way, but is this really the case? There are three points that are missing from the thought-for-thought translation:

In the scriptures, "sleep" is used metaphorically as death, also inferring a temporary state where one will wake again, or be resurrected. That idea is lost in the thought-for-thought translation. (Ps 13:3; John 11:11-14; Ac 7:60; 1Co 7:39; 15:51; 1Th 4:13)

Sleeping with or lying down with his father also conveys the idea of having closed his life and having found favor in God's eyes as did his forefathers.

When we leave out some of the words from the original, we also leave out the possibility of more meaning being drawn from the text. Missing is the word *shakab* ("to lie down" or "to sleep"), *'im* ("with") and 'ab in the plural ("forefathers"). Below are verses that enhance our understanding of death, by way of sleep, as being temporary for those who will be awakened by a resurrection.

Psalm 13:3 Updated American Standard Version (UASV)

³ Consider and answer me, Jehovah my God;
  give light to my eyes
lest I sleep *the sleep of* death,

John 11:11-14 Updated American Standard Version (UASV)

¹¹ After saying these things, he said to them, "Our friend Lazarus has fallen asleep, but I go to awaken him." ¹² The disciples said to him, "Lord, if he has fallen asleep, he will get well." ¹³ Now Jesus had spoken of his death, but they thought that he meant taking rest in sleep. ¹⁴ Then Jesus told them plainly, "Lazarus has died,

Acts 7:60 Updated American Standard Version (UASV)

⁶⁰ Then falling on his knees, he cried out with a loud voice, "Lord, do not hold this sin against them!" Having said this, he fell asleep.¹⁵

---

¹⁵ I.e. died

1 Corinthians 7:39 Updated American Standard Version (UASV)

³⁹ A wife is bound for so long time as her husband is alive. But if her husband should fall asleep (*koimethe*) [in death], she is free to be married to whom she wishes, only in the Lord.¹⁶

1 Corinthians 15:51 Updated American Standard Version (UASV)

⁵¹ Behold, I tell you a mystery; we will not all sleep, but we will all be changed,

1 Thessalonians 4:13 Updated American Standard Version (UASV)

¹³ But we do not want you to be ignorant,¹⁷ brothers, about those who are asleep, so that you will not grieve as do the rest who have no hope.

Those who argue for a thought-for-thought translation will say the literal translation "slept" or "lay down" is no longer a way of expressing death in the modern English-speaking world. While this may be true to some extent, the context of chapter two, verse 1: "when David was about to die" and the latter half of 2:10: "was buried in the city of David" resolves that issue. Moreover, while the reader may have to meditate a little longer, or indulge him/herself in the culture of different Biblical times, they will not be deprived of the full potential that a verse has to convey. (Grudem, et al. 2005, pp. 20-21)

---

¹⁶ The ASV, ESV, NASB, and other literal translation do not hold true to their literal translation philosophy here. This does not bode well in their claim that literal is the best policy. We are speaking primarily to the ESV translators, who make this claim in numerous books.

¹⁷ Or *uninformed*

A Word of Caution

The dynamic equivalent and paraphrase can and does obscure things from the reader by overreaching in their translations. This can be demonstrated on the moral standards found in 1 Corinthians 6:9-10.

1 Corinthians 6:9-10 The Message

9-10 Don't you realize that this is not the way to live? Unjust people who don't care about God will not be joining in his kingdom. Those who use and abuse each other, use and abuse sex, use and abuse the earth and everything in it, don't qualify as citizens in God's kingdom.

1 Corinthians 6:9-10 Updated American Standard Version (UASV)

9 Or do you not know that the unrighteous will not inherit the kingdom of God? Do not be deceived; neither fornicators, nor idolaters, nor adulterers, nor men of passive homosexual acts, nor men of active homosexual acts,[18] 10 nor thieves, nor the covetous, nor drunkards, nor revilers, nor swindlers, will inherit the kingdom of God.

If you compare the MSG with the UASV, you will notice that the MSG does not even list the specifics defined by the apostle Paul on precisely what kind of conduct we should shun.

Matthew 7:13 Today's English Version (TEV)

13"Go in through the narrow gate, because the gate to **hell** is wide and the road that leads to it is easy, and there are many who travel it.

---

[18] The two Greek terms refer to passive men partners and active men partners in consensual homosexual acts

Matthew 7:13 Updated American Standard Version (UASV)

[13] "Enter through the narrow gate; for the gate is wide and the way is broad that leads to **destruction**, and there are many who enter through it.

The Greek word *apōleian* means "destruction," "waste," "annihilation," "ruin." Therefore, one has to ask, 'why did the TEV translation committee render it "hell"? It has all the earmarks of theological bias. The translation committee is looking to promote the doctrine of eternal torment, not destruction. The objective of the translator is to render it the way that it should be rendered. If it supports a certain doctrine, this should be accepted, if not, then this should be accepted as well. The policy is that God does not need an overzealous translator to convey his doctrinal message.

1 Corinthians 11:10

10 διὰ   τοῦτο ὀφείλει ἡ γυνὴ ἐξουσίαν ἔχειν ἐπὶ τῆς
    Through this   owes the woman authority to have on the

κεφαλῆς   διὰ   τοὺς ἀγγέλους
head   because of the messengers

Literal	Dynamic Equivalent	Dynamic Equivalent
1 Corinthians 11:10 (UASV)	1 Corinthians 11:10 (GNT)	1 Corinthians 11:10 (CEV)
[10] This is why the woman ought to have a symbol of authority on her head, because of the angels.	[10] On account of the angels, then, a woman should have a covering over her head to show that she is under her	[10] And so, because of this, and also because of the angels, a woman ought to wear something on

	husband's authority.	her head, as a sign of her authority.

As we can see, the English lexical glosses of the interlinear are literally carried over into the Source Language word for word, keeping the exact form. This is called a **gloss** in the world of the Bible translator. While this does not convey much meaning to the average English reader, it does to one who has studied Biblical Greek. However, the Bible student would have a literal translation as a study Bible. The literal translation, as you can see, will keep the form as far as is possible, as well as the wording. The Dynamic Equivalent advocates will argue that this does not sound natural. Well, for those that want the Word of God in its undiluted form, as accurately as possible, we will accept a little unnatural sounding at times. Soon, we will see the danger of going beyond translation into interpretation.

Our literal translation contains ambiguity. Is the writer talking about *women* or *wives*? Is the woman to have her own authority, or is something or someone else to have authority over her? This is just fine, because it ambiguity has many benefits, as you will see. First, as a quick aside, the work of interpretation will weed out those pseudo-Christians, who do not want to put any effort into their relationship with God, who do not want to buy out the time to understand. Now, the reader has the right to determine for himself or herself which is the correct interpretation. The translator should not steal this right from them, for the translator or the translation committee, could be wrong, and life or death may be uncertain.

Seeing two dynamic equivalents side-by-side helps you to see that they have arrived at two different conclusions and both cannot be right. The *Today's English Version* believes that the "woman" here is really the "wife," as it refers to the "husband." It also believes that the wife is to be under the husband's authority. On the other hand, the *Contemporary English Version* does not commit to the argument of "woman" versus "wife," but does understand the verse to mean the woman has her *own* authority. She has the authority to act as she feels she should, as long as she wears something as a sign of this.

A good translation will do the following:

(1) Accurately render the original language words and style into the corresponding English word and style that were inspired by God.

(2) Translate the meaning of words literally, when the wording and construction of the original text allow for such a rendering in the target language.

(3) Transfer the correct meaning (sense) of a word or a phrase when a literal rendering of the original-language word or a phrase would garble or obscure the meaning.

(4) After considering, the objectives of the first three points, as far as possible, use natural, easy-to-understand language that inspires reading.

Are there such translations available on the market? Yes, the author recommends that you use the NASB Zondervan Study Bible by Kenneth L. Barker, Donald W. Burdick, John H. Stek and Walter W. Wessel (Jan 6, 2000), as your primary study Bible. Of course, you should consider other literal translations as time permits. In addition, use the dynamic equivalents as mini-commentaries, as that is what they are.

CHAPTER 7 The Different Kinds of Bible Translations

Word-for-Word *Translation Philosophy* (literal) translation seeks to render the original language words and style into a corresponding English word and style. Again, they seek to retain the original syntax and sentence structure, and the style of each writer as far as possible.

Thought-for-Thought Translation Philosophy (dynamic equivalent) seeks to render the biblical meaning of the original language text as accurately as possible into an English informal (conversational) equivalent.

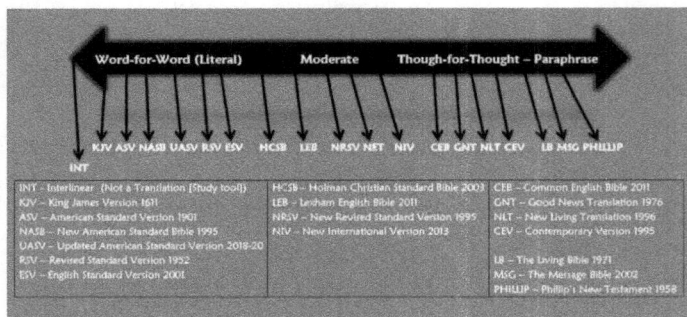

Of course, as any translation continuum chart will show, many translations fall throughout this spectrum. For example, the ASV and the NASB are more literal than say the ESV, and the ESV is more literal than the HCSB, while the HCSB is more literal than the NIV or the NRSV. On the other side of the spectrum, the MSG and TLB are a paraphrase instead of a translation than say the NLT, CEV, or TEV (GNT). In addition, you have the NIV trying to work right in the middle of these two philosophies. Moreover, if you are still following the picture, the HCSB attempts to fall between the NIV and the ESV. Both of these translation philosophies have their strengths and weaknesses if the translator goes to the extreme in either direction. However, the dynamic equivalent translation philosophy has weaknesses and dangers that are harmful to the student of God's Word.

The main strengths of the literal translation are that they are trying to preserve the original text, the ancient expressions, how the words are joined together and rendering the words consistently. All of this allows the reader to determine what the meaning is, and not have to depend on the translator to do his work for him. This also ties the Bible together as a whole, and the reader is better able see the Old Testament in the New Testament. The main strengths of the thought-for-thought translation are simply that they get the meaning immediately, as would have the original readers. As the original readers would not have had to struggle with grammar and syntax, or idiomatic expressions, so it is too, the modern reader of a thought-for-thought translation has all of these points of concern modernized for them in an easy to read translation. At first glance, this may appear like an ideal approach.

Those who favor the thought-for-thought form of translation abuse the statement that "all translation is interpretation." Dr. Leland Ryken has touched on this, saying, "There is only one sense in which all translation is interpretation, and it is not what dynamic equivalent translators usually mean by their cliché. All translation is lexical or linguistic interpretation. That is, translators must decide what English word or phrase most closely corresponds to a given word of the original text. I myself do not believe that "interpretation" is the best word by which to name this process, but inasmuch as it requires a "judgment call" on the part of translators, there is something akin to interpretation when translators decide whether, for example, the Israelites were led through the wilderness or the desert." [19]

The translator should not go beyond the "lexical or linguistic interpretation" that Ryland speaks of unless there are very good reasons for doing so, such as a verse that would be unintelligible. When the translator goes beyond into the realms of interpretation, i.e., explaining the literal meaning, "wear fine clothes, with a splash of cologne, in place of "Let your garments be always white. Let not oil be lacking on your head." (Eccl. 9:8) What readers are not being told is, when a translator or committee makes these interpretive changes, he is removing the reader from the equation. In other words, there is no need for the reader to concern himself with understanding how to interpret the Word of God correctly, as it has already been done for him.

Perception of Today's Readers

The reader of God's Word, be they young children, teenagers, the elderly, or ones with learning disabilities, they need to see as the structure and meaning of the original, by way of corresponding English words and phrases, and sentence patterns. The original word of God needs to be transparent to the reader. The reader needs to be brought up to the translation, not have the translation dumbed down. The focus of the literal translation is the Word of God in the original, so we know that what we have is the Word of God, not the word of man. The focus of the dynamic equivalent is on the reader. Below are some examples of how the dynamic equivalent perceives today's readers.

- "After ascertaining as accurately as possible the meaning of the original, the translator's next task

---

[19] (Ryken, Choosing a Bible: Understanding Bible Translation Differences 2005)

was to express that meaning in a manner and form easily understood by the readers" – GNB.

- "Metaphorical language is often difficult for contemporary readers to understand, so at times we have chosen to translate or illuminate the metaphor" – NLT.

- "Because for most readers today the phrase 'the Lord of hosts' and 'God of hosts' have ittle meaning, this version renders them 'the Lord Almighty' and God Almighty'" – NIV.

- "Ancient customs are often unfamiliar to modern readers" – NCV.

- "We have used the vocabulary and language structures . . . of a junior high student" – NLT.

- "The Contemporary English Version has been described as a 'user-friendly' and 'mission-driven' translation that can be read aloud without stumbling, heard without misunderstanding, and listened to with enjoyment and appreciation because the language is contemporary and the style is lucid and lyrical."

Eugene Nida, the father of thought-for-thought translation, had this to say about literal translators in *Christianity Today*: "This 'word worship' helps people to have confidence, but they don't understand the text. And as long as they worship words, instead of worshiping God as revealed in Jesus Christ, they feel safe."[20] The real facts are that Nida and of his Dynamic Equivalent camp worship the modern reader instead of respecting the Author of the Bible and his Word choices. Bible scholar John MacArthur states: thought-for-thought translations "diminish the glory

---

[20] Nida, Eugene: Meaning-full Translations. Christianity Today, October 7, 2002: 46-49.

of divine revelation by being more concerned with the human reader than the divine author."

The thought-for-thought proponents have gone beyond translation by modifying words that they feel to be too difficult for the modern reader to comprehend; to taking the metaphorical language of say 2 Kings 2:7: "Then the captain on whose hand the king leaned said to the man of God ..." (ESV), to 'the personal attendant of the king said to Elisha ..." (GNB). Rather than even modernize the idea of the ancient custom of kings or men of authority to lean on the hand or arm of a servant or one in an inferior position, they simply removed this thought from God's word. They also assume ignorance on the part of the modern-day reader by taking statements that they believe would be misunderstood and expressing them to be easily understood. In addition, they have removed gender language they feel offensive, as one will see from their evaluation of the TNIV.

Literal Translation	Dynamic Equivalent
1 Timothy 6:17 Updated American Standard Version (UASV) [17] Instruct those who are rich in the present age not to be arrogant, and to place their hope, not on uncertain riches, but on God, who richly provides us with all the things to enjoy;	**1 Timothy 6:17** New Living Translation (NLT) [17] Teach those who are rich in this world not to be proud and not to trust in their money, which is so unreliable. Their trust should be in God, who richly gives us all we need for our enjoyment.
1 Timothy **6:17** New American Standard Bible (NASB)	1 Timothy **6:17** Contemporary English Version (**CEV**)

¹⁷ Instruct those who are rich in this present world not to be conceited or to fix their hope on the uncertainty of riches, but on God, who richly supplies us with all things to enjoy.	¹⁷ Warn the rich people of this world not to be proud or to trust in wealth that is easily lost. Tell them to have faith in God, who is rich and blesses us with everything we need to enjoy life.

Why do both the NLT and the CEV feel the need to add words that are not in the Greek text: "we need"? Is it because they feel the inexperienced reader will abuse the text? Is there some liberal progressive mindset that cannot allow a person to have more than what *they need*? Paul is simply stating that we can enjoy *all* of God's creation, not just what *we need*.

| James 3:1-2 Updated American Standard Version (UASV)

3 Not many of you should become teachers, my brothers, knowing that we shall receive heavier judgment. ² For we all stumble²¹ in many ways. If | James 3:1-2 New American Standard Bible (NASB)

3 Let not many *of you* become teachers, my brethren, knowing that as such we will incur a stricter judgment. ² For we all stumble in many *ways*. If anyone does not stumble in what he says, he is a perfect man, able | James 3:1-2 Christian Standard Bible (CSB)

3 Not many should become teachers, my brothers, because you know that we will receive a stricter judgment. ² For we all stumble in many ways. If anyone does not stumble in what he says, he is mature, able also |
|---|---|---|

---

²¹ Or "make mistakes."

anyone does not stumble in what he says,[22] he is a perfect man, able also to bridle his whole body.	to bridle the whole body as well.	to control the whole body.

James 3:1-2 The Message (MSG)

[1-2]Don't be in any rush to become a teacher, my friends. Teaching is highly responsible work. Teachers are held to the strictest standards. And none of us is perfectly qualified. We get it wrong nearly every time we open our mouths. If you could find someone whose speech was perfectly true, you'd have a perfect person, in perfect control of life.

Okay, raise your hand if you want to trust the Bible after reading in The Message paraphrase that James and other teachers like the apostles *get it wrong nearly every time we open our mouths.* We could go on and on with literally hundreds of examples of the changes that go into God's word by means of these creative translators, who 'get it wrong nearly every time they translate.' The last comment was meant as comedic sarcasm and is a bit of an exaggeration.

Our example texts below are well chosen as they demonstrate the differences in translation principles. Keep in mind that the ESV is an essentially literal translation, and its translation team has penned numerous books and articles emphasizing the value of the essentially literal approach, yet at the same time, it tends to abandon that

---

[22] Lit., "*word*"

approach all too quickly and runs to the dynamic equivalent philosophy. After we read the texts below, let us ask what a tutor is. Does our modern-day understanding of tutor correspond with what Paul meant? Did the Galatians have a different understanding of a tutor? Does "guardian" or "charge" solve the problem? Well, read the texts below. After reading the text, reflect on what each translation accomplished. After the ASV and the NASB's use of "tutor," did we get the impression that the law was a teacher? And what happened to that impression after reading the ESV? What about after the NIRV, did it cloud our mental grasp up even more? Then, look at the notes below that.

Galatians 3:23-25 Updated American Standard Version (UASV)	Galatians 3:23-25 New American Standard Bible (NASB)	Galatians 3:23-25 English Standard Version (ESV)
23 But before faith came, we were kept in custody under the law, being shut up to the faith which was later to be revealed 24 Therefore the Law has become our tutor23 to lead us to Christ, so that we may be justified by faith. 25 But now that faith has come, we are no longer under a tutor.	23 But before faith came, we were kept in custody under the law, being shut up to the faith which was later to be revealed. 24 Therefore the Law has become our tutor *to lead us* to Christ, so that we may be justified by	23 Now before faith came, we were held captive under the law, imprisoned until the coming faith would be revealed. 24 So then, the law was our guardian until Christ came, in order that we might be justified by

---

23 Lit *pedagogue*; Gr *paidagogos*. The tutor in Bible times was not the teacher but rather a guardian who led the student to the teacher.

	faith. [25] But now that faith has come, we are no longer under a tutor.	faith. [25] But now that faith has come, we are no longer under a guardian,

Galatians 3:23-25 New International Reader's Version (NIRV)

[23] Before faith in Christ came, we were held prisoners by the law. We were locked up until faith was made known. [24] So the law was put in charge until Christ came. He came so that we might be made right with God by believing in Christ. [25] But now faith in Christ has come. So we are no longer under the control of the law.

Literal Translation: The literal translation will bring over from the Greek [*paidagogos*, tutor], the structure of the original text (SL) and the presupposition pool[24] of the author and original readers. However, if understanding would be next to impossible, only then would the literal translation step over to the interpretive translation.

Dynamic Equivalent: The dynamic equivalent, the thought-for-thought translation will take the structure of the original and the presupposition pool of the original author and reader ["tutor"] and will bring it over into the structure and presupposition pool of the modern reader "guardian." Nevertheless, the rendering of "guardian" is actually a somewhat correct interpretation, unlike the NIRV "control."

> 1: a tutor i.e. a guardian and guide of boys. Among the Greeks and the Romans the name was applied to trustworthy slaves who were charged with the duty of supervising the life and

---

[24] A presupposition pool is the common knowledge and understanding of a particular time, place, language, culture and religion.

morals of boys belonging to the better class. The boys were not allowed so much as to step out of the house without them before arriving at the age of manhood.[25]

However, does "guardian" help us any more than did "tutor"? Yes, it would, but it is not the complete picture. In addition, a person reading "tutor" would tend to think in a modern way and come home with the idea that the "law" was a teacher in some way. This would be incomplete too. Like the childhood tutor of the first-century, the Mosaic Law was a guardian that protected the Israelites from their surrounding neighbors until the arrival of Christ. Like the guardian of boys, the Law [tutor] also taught some lessons about life along the way, as well as disciplining the child. There is no doubt that upon the Exodus from Egypt, one would view the nation of Israel as nothing other than a child, in a world of raptorial nations and people.

There is no doubt that the Bible is simple and easy to understand at times, but this is very rare, it is far more often than not: extremely complex, difficult and sophisticated. Consider,

Isaiah 38:12-13 English Standard Version (ESV)

[12] My dwelling is plucked up and removed from me
   like a shepherd's tent;
like a weaver I have rolled up my life;
   he cuts me off from the loom;
from day to night you bring me to an end;
[13]   I calmed myself until morning;
like a lion he breaks all my bones;
   from day to night you bring me to an end.

---

[25] Strong, James: The Exhaustive Concordance of the Bible: Showing Every Word of the Text of the Common English Version of the Canonical Books, and Every Occurrence of Each Word in Regular Order. electronic ed. Ontario: Woodside Bible Fellowship., 1996, S. G3807

Why So Many New Translations?

The last 60-years have seen the release of one new English Bible translation after another. Here we go again as if we need another translation! It has become quite the big business to keep putting out the latest, updated, new version, a new translation. However, it goes even deeper than that, because we now have: church Bibles and ministry Bibles, family Bibles, study Bibles, topical Bibles, apologetic Bibles, audience geared Bibles, and so on. In addition, one can now determine where they want their Bible to be on the scale of just how literal it is.

After making the point that there seems to be no end to the line of new English translations, it must be said that there will always be a need for new translations. 'Why' you may be asking? If we were to turn to the many translators in the field of Bible translation, they would offer at least three good reasons: (1) the manuscripts that have been discovered over the centuries are always being studied and better understood, and this increased knowledge may mean adjustments in the translation. (2) Our knowledge of the Bible languages just keeps improving over the years, and once again this can lead to more accurate translations. (3) Languages are living and growing and change over time, altering the meaning of words, in some case, to the opposite. In 1611, "let" in "I let John go to school" meant "stop" or "restrain."

Translating the Word of God is No Easy Task

While it is true that technology may have made the task somewhat easier, it still takes years to bring a translation to the market. Some things that most may have not considered are (1) the method, process, tools, and sources that will be used to make the translation (2) who is the audience that the translation will be directed toward (the target audience); and (3) what type of translation is it to be: literal (UASV, NASB), dynamic equivalent (NLT, TEV), or something in between (NIV, NJB)? Below we will take a brief look at each of these.

What are the Sources behind the Translation?

Many, who are aware that there are Hebrew and Greek manuscripts used in Bible translation, are not aware of their extent. As some may also know, there is not one single manuscript of the original Hebrew Old Testament or the Greek New Testament still in existence. Yet, there are thousands of copied manuscripts of the original language Old Testament and New Testament, and thousands of copies of it in other languages, as well as quotations from the early church Fathers. Are these what the modern translator will consider? Yes, they are a part of the tools within their tool chest, but some of the world's leading scholars have already considered them extensively for 200-years. In this, they have created a critical text[26] for both testaments.

Today's translation committees have access to a number of critical texts. However, most modern English translations depend on the Masoretic text of the Hebrew Bible as found in the BHS *Biblia Hebraica Stuttgartensia* (2nd ed., 1983), and the Greek text as found in the WH NU *Westcott and Hort* of 1881 and the Nestle-Aland Greek New Testament (28th ed., 2011), as well as the *United Bible Societies* (5th edition, 2011). The work is far faster today

---

[26] Critical should not to be misconstrued in a negative sense in this instance. It involves comments and opinions that analyze are judging each word of the Old or New Testament as being original or not, in an extremely detailed way, which we do not have time to cover herein. For an introduction in textual studies, see the end of the article under Resources for Additional Research.

than 50 years ago, as the translator, today has access to Bible software as well as internet access.

Target Audience – Who is it?

In the days of the Tyndale-King James Version, where one translation served the purpose of the many, this would seem to be a strange question. However, for any who have ventured in the bookstore to pick out a Bible, it is immediately clear. You have a church Bible, a family Bible, a Children's Bible, a study Bible, an archaeological study Bible and many others. One might ask, 'why can we not just have one Bible for everyone?'

The Dynamic Equivalent translator would argue that the scholar must have a translation that is targeted to him (NASB, UAS); the teacher must have a translation (ESV) while his Bible student must have another (NIV), and the churchgoer yet another (NLT). In the house, the father may have a specific form of translation (NIV), while the wife another (NIV Women's Bible), and the teenager his own (NIV Teen Bible, TNIV), with the younger children still yet another (NIV Boy's Bible, The Action Bible, My Little Bible). Then, there is also the African American Bibles. The questions are simple, are the Bibles to be adapted to the people needs, or are the people expected to adapt to the Bible?

Even the Plowboy Should Have Bible

William Tyndale (1494 – 1536), brought us our first printed English Bible. His translation philosophy would be followed for the next 420 years. His objective audience was all English speaking people. On one occasion, Tyndale, heard an educated man say that it would be better to be without God's law than without the law of the Pope. Tyndale answered "I defy the Pope and all his laws. If God spare my life, ere many years I will cause a boy that drives the plough to know more of the Scripture, than he does." Tyndale's translation of the Greek New Testament was easy enough for a plowboy to understand in his time. However, does this mean that he dumbed down the translation so that the plowboy could easily understand the Bible?

No, Tyndale did not produce a translation to appease the needs of the plowboy; he expected the plowboy to buy out the time, to make an effort to be able to understand God's Word. He made no adjustments; his translation was informal when that was the case with the original, and formal when that was the case as well. At times, his translation ranges from complex to highly complex. Tyndale translated what the original text said, not what he determined it meant. Unlike: Ps 24:4 (ESV) He who has clean hands and a pure heart; Ps 24:4 (CEV) only those who do right for the right reasons; or Phil 4:1 (ESV) my joy and crown; Phil 4:7 (TEV) How happy you make me, and how proud I am of you. Tyndale did not give way to the less educated, even though that was the largest portion of the population at the time. He expected the less-educated to grow in their understanding of the English language.

The Type of Translation

What is the method of translating the critical texts of the Old and New Testament that the translation committee will follow as they produce their new Bible translation? Will the committee use other translations as their foundational text; if so, how closely will these be followed? Other translation committees may choose to make a completely new revision. If it were the former, an example would be the 1946-1952 Revised Standard Version (RSV), which is a revision of the 1901 American Standard Version (ASV). The RSV would have had the intentions of removing the archaic language and correcting any inaccuracies. Another example would be the 1990

New Revised Standard Version (NRSV), a revision of the Revised Standard Version. Both the ASV and the RSV continued in the translation philosophy of William Tyndale, sometimes with the exact wording. Sadly, the NRSV has abandoned those principles, which makes it a considerably less literal translation.

If the committee is following the latter and producing a new translation, completely from the original language texts; it would still consider other translations. However, it would give most of its attention to the BHK and BHS for the Old Testament[27] and the WH, UBS5, NA28 for the New Testament.[28] Other tools would be textual commentaries, Hebrew and Greek dictionaries, grammars, exegetical commentaries, translation handbooks, special investigations, and so on. Many translators that have had experience in the field of translation would certainly prefer to produce a new translation, as opposed to making a revision.

Another choice that comes before those producing this new or revised translation is the option of a literal translation or a Dynamic Equivalent (or functional) translation. The literal translation has the aim to capture the accurate wording of the original text and the personal style of each Bible writer, as far as possible. In other words, they want to reproduce what the Bible writer penned in both word and style. The Dynamic Equivalent method seeks to transmit interpretive opinions of the original text, focusing on the message. The literal translation is focused on the reproduction of the text, and the Dynamic Equivalent translation is focused on the reader.

If the Bible translation committee is commissioned to do a literal translation, they must then determine just how

---

[27] "BHK" refers to Kittel's Biblia Hebraica and "BHS" refers to Biblia Hebraica Stuttgartensia.

[28] "WH" refers to The New Testament in the Original Greek. "UBS" refers to The Greek New Testament, by United Bible Societies. "NA" refers to the Nestle-Aland Greek Text.

literal the translation will be, without sacrificing the sense of the original. Another concern is the consistency of the rendering of the words in the original. If **the context permits**, each time a Hebrew or Greek word appears, the same word should be given to it in the translation. Another aspect of the team is that they must try to capture the different styles of the New Testament writers. The 27 books of the New Testament consist of multiple writers that all have distinct ways of writing. For instance, the gospel writers Matthew, Mark, and Luke, cover Jesus' life and ministry but differ in the words they choose to use and the arrangement of those words. Mark writes a fresh and natural Greek of high quality. He tends to keep it simple but certainly animated and exciting. Luke, on the other hand, has the pen of a professional, using terms that show he is far more careful about small details. His being a physician is the reason for his extensive use of medical terms. He also appears to be very familiar with seafaring, as is evidenced by Acts 27-28. Matthew appears to be in between Mark and Luke when it comes to style.

There is a complication to maintaining the style of a given author, as he may change his style. Being that the Apostle Paul has penned far more books than the other New Testament writers have, he is the most noted for this. A professor of classical languages, who is also a member of the Swedish Bible Committee, comments on this, "He has an enormous register: elevated prose poem as in 1 Corinthians 13, moving eloquence as in Romans 8:31-39, but also dry explanations. . . . His vocabulary is great (900 words that are specific only to him). He was a brilliant master of speech."

The NET Bible (New English Translation) has over 60,000 translator notes; while other translations have over 10,000 footnotes to help the reader better understand their Bible. The footnotes are used further to explain such areas as custom and culture, textual problems, translation issues, original language words, basic language meanings, valuable alternative renderings. Also, the meaning of names of Bible books, persons, and places, as well as geographical data. Money, weights, measures, and calendar dates are converted into modern terms. Obviously, this would take extensive research, aside from the translation itself. Moreover, these are just a few of the problems that are faced when one contemplates a new translation. Some of the other basics that most may not consider are the text on the pages, the organization of chapters and verses, the font, and so on.

The Need for New Translations

If the gospel is to be preached in all the earth, new translations are always going to be necessary, in many languages. Yet, as was demonstrated in the above, this is no easy task. The labor involved in such a task takes years, and by dozens of people, even with today's technology. The need for new English translations is not really as paramount. The ones that we have are more than we could ever need, and only need to be revised and updated periodically.

CHAPTER 8 The Making of a Worthy Translation

Exactly why are we producing and publishing other translations beyond the King James Version of 1611? The King James Version has been the primary translation of the Christian community for 400 years (1611-2011). There is no doubt that this Bible alone has affected the lives of hundreds of millions and has influenced the principles in Bible translation for the past four centuries.

Before we delve into what makes for a good translation, let us pause to consider the translation policy of the KJV translation committee. We can hardly talk about the KJV without looking at the translator William Tyndale (1494-1536), the man who published the first printed New Testament from the original language of Greek. In the face of much persecution, William Tyndale of England followed with his English translation of Erasmus' Greek New Testament text, completing this while in exile on the continent of Europe in 1525.

Tyndale respected and treasured the Bible. However, in his days, the religious leaders insisted on keeping it in Latin, a language that had been dead for centuries. Therefore, with the purpose of making it available to his fellow citizens, Tyndale was determined to translate the Bible into English. While the idea of Bible translation being against the law may be unfamiliar to the modern mind, this was not the case in Tyndale's day. He was educated at Oxford University and became an esteemed instructor at The Cambridge University. Because of his desire to bring the common man the Bible in English, he had to flee from his academic career, escaping the Continent. His life became one of a fugitive, but he managed to complete the New Testament and some of the Old Testament, before he was finally arrested, imprisoned for heresy, and strangled at the stake, with his body being burned afterward.

Tyndale's work sparked a widespread translation project that produced a new revision every couple of years, or so it seemed. The Coverdale Bible of 1536, the Matthew's Bible of 1537, the Great Bible of 1539, the Taverner's Bible of 1539, the Geneva Bible of 1560 (went through 140 editions), the Edmund Becke's Bible of 1549, the Bishop's Bible of 1568, and the Rheims-Douay Bible of 1610. The King James Version is a revision of all these translations, as they too were of their predecessor, the Tyndale translation. The KJV translation committee was ordered to use the Bishop's Bible as their foundation text and was not to alter it unless Tyndale, Coverdale, Matthew, Cranmer or the Great Bible, and the Geneva agreed, and then they were to assume that reading. Thus, the King James Version is unquestionably 90 percent William Tyndale's translation.

There is no other translation, which possesses more literary beauty than the King James Version. However, there are several reasons as to why there was a need to revise the King James Version. The **first reason** is its textual basis, which is from the period of 1611. The Greek text behind the KJV New Testament is what is known as the Textus Receptus, a corrupt Greek text produced by a scholar in the 16th-century, Desiderius Erasmus. Concerning this text, Dr. Bruce Metzger wrote that it was "a handful of late and haphazardly collected minuscule manuscripts and in a dozen passages its reading is supported by no Greek witnesses." (Metzger 2003, 106) While most of the corruptions are considered insignificant, others are significant, such as 1 Timothy 3:16; 1 John 5:7; John 7:53-8:11; and Mark 16:9-20. However, we cannot lay the blame at the feet of the translation committee of the KJV, for they did not have the textual evidence that we possess today.

The **second reason** is that it comes from the 17th-century and contains many archaic words that either obscure the meaning or mislead its reader: "howbeit," "thee," "thy," "thou," "thine," and "shambles." An example of misleading can be found in the word "let," which meant to "stop," "hinder" or "restrain" in 1611, but today means "to allow" or "to permit." Therefore, when the KJV says that Paul 'let the great apostasy come into the church,' it is completely misleading to the modern mind. In 1611 "let" meant that he 'restrained or prevented the apostasy.' (2 Thess. 2:7) The KJV at Mark 6:20 inform us "Herod feared John, knowing that he was a just man and an holy, and observed him." Actually, the Greek behind "observed him" means that Herod "kept him safe."

The **third reason** is that the KJV contains translation errors. However, like the first reason, it is not the fault of the translators, as Hebrew and Greek were just resurfacing as subjects of serious study after the Dark Ages. The discovery of papyrus writings in Egypt, in the late 19th and early 20th centuries, has helped us better to understand the common (Koine) Greek of the first century C.E. These discoveries have shown that everyday words were not understood as well as had been thought. The KJV at Matthew 5:22 informs the reader "whosoever is angry with his brother without a cause shall be in danger of the judgment: and whosoever shall say to his brother, Raca, shall be in danger of the council ..." The ESV renders it, "whoever insults his brother will be liable (a term of abuse) to the council ..." Scholar Walter C. Kaiser has said, "the actual insult mentioned by Jesus is the word 'Raca' as it stands in the KJV. The precise meaning of 'Raca' is disputed; it is probably an Aramaic word meaning something like 'imbecile,' but was plainly regarded as a deadly insult."

The translators that have come after the King James Version can draw much direction in what makes a worthy translation by considering the principles of translation that were followed in the production of the world's most influential Bible. The translators endeavored to discover the corresponding English word for the actual original language word of Hebrew and Greek.

According to Alister McGrath, the translators felt obligated to . . .

1) Ensure that every word in the original was rendered by an English equivalent;
2) Make it clear when they added any words to make the sense clearer, or to lead to better English syntax. . . .
3) Follow the basic word order of the original wherever possible.[29]

A Worthy Translation is an Accurate Translation

If asked what the number one priority in translation is, most translators would argue that the biggest responsibility is *accuracy*. However, if this conversation were between a translator of a literal or verbal corresponding (word-for-word) mindset and one of the thought-for-thought (sense-for-sense, meaning-based) mindset, the next question would be, 'what do you mean by *accuracy*?' The thought-for-thought translator would most certainly say, 'to render the Biblical *meaning* of the original language text as *accurately* as possible into English.' The literal side would return with, 'to render the *words and style* of the original language text into a corresponding English equivalent word or phrase as *accurately* as possible.' The dynamic equivalent translator is attempting to re-express what they believe the original language text *meant* into English, removing the need of interpretive reading for the modern-

---

[29] McGrath, Alister. *In the Beginning: The Story of the King James Bible and How It Changed a Nation, a Language, and a Culture.* New York: Anchor, 2002, p. 250.

day Bible student; the literal translator wants to re-express what the original language text says into a corresponding English equivalent, leaving it up to the reader, to determine the meaning for himself.[30]

How does the Bible reader know what the Bible means if they do not know what it says? If the reader is given what a translator has determined the meaning as, and not what it says, how does the reader determine its meaning as being accurate? Are they not shortchanging the reader from the right of having access to the very words of God; but instead, feeding them a regurgitated interpretation of what another thinks it means?

A word-for-word corresponding equivalent translator expects the reader to ascertain the meaning of the words that were used by studying and researching the text; with helps of course: word-study dictionaries, lexicons, commentaries, and the use of exegetical principles, as well as by the Christian person who is carrying out a Bible study with them. Many sense-for-sense translators actually believe that the reader is too ignorant and too lazy to ascertain the meaning by study and reaching within those helps, so they provide it for them. If the reader has the meaning already in front of him by way of the translator, he has no way of getting back to what the texts say, to determine if the meaning is, in fact, correct. All translators know that there is theological bias in all of us, and we will at times, bend things to have it our way. Looking at the worst-case situation first, some translators violate grammar and syntax to get a theologically important verse to read according to their doctrinal position, and we are to trust them to give us a translation already interpreted for us?

---

[30] "The translator must re-express the meaning of the original message as exactly as possible in the language to which he is translating." (Barnwell 1975, 23) "a translation that strives to translate the exact words of the original-language text in a translation, but not in such a rigid way as to violate the normal rules of language and syntax in the receptor language." (Ryken 2002, 19)

1 John 2:5, 15; 3:17; 4:9; 5:3 (New American Standard Bible)	1 John 2:5, 15; 3:17; 4:9; 5:3 (New International Version)	1 John 2:5, 15; 3:17; 4:9; 5:3 (New Living Translation)
in him the *love of God* has truly been perfected	*love for God* is truly made complete	. . . obey God's word truly show how completely they *love him*
If anyone loves the world, the *love of the Father* is not in him	If anyone loves the world, *love for the Father* is not in them	when you love the world, you do not have the *love of the Father*
how does the *love of God* abide in him	how can the *love of God* be in that person	how can *God's love* be in that person
By this the *love of God* was manifested in us	This is how *God showed his* love among us	*God showed* how much he loved us
For this is the love of God, that we keep His commandments	this is *love for God*: to keep his commands	Loving God means keeping his commandments

"Love of God" and "love of the Father," what did the apostle John mean when he penned those words? Was he referring to the *love that God has for us*, or to our *love for God*, or the *love* that comes *from God* and is *expressed through us* to others? B. F. Westcott understood this to mean "the love that God has made known," while F. F. Bruce came to an opposite conclusion: as meaning "our love for God."[31] The reader of John's epistle would have

---

[31] B. F. Westcott, Epistles of St. John, 48-49; F. F. Bruce, *The Epistles of John.* Grand Rapids, MI: Eerdmans, 1970, 51-2.

had to determine what John meant by the words that he used. Today's reader should be given the same opportunity and responsibility; he must determine what was meant by the corresponding English words in a literal translation. The sense-for-sense dynamic equivalent translations have come to opposite conclusions, meaning that both cannot be right. Therefore, it is best that the reader be given what was said, and carry the responsibility of determining what was meant by what was said.

Romans 8:35-39 Updated American Standard Version (UASV)	Romans 8:35-39 The Message (MSG)
35 Who will separate us from the love of Christ? Will tribulation, or distress, or persecution, or famine, or nakedness, or danger, or sword? 36 As it is written, "For your sake we are being put to death all day long; we are considered as sheep to be slaughtered." 37 But in all these things we are more than conquerors through the one having loved us. 38 For I am convinced that neither death, nor life, nor angels, nor rulers, nor things present, nor things to come, nor powers, 39 nor height, nor depth, nor any other created thing,	31-39 So, what do you think? With God on our side like this, how can we lose? If God didn't hesitate to put everything on the line for us, embracing our condition and exposing himself to the worst by sending his own Son, is there anything else he wouldn't gladly and freely do for us? And who would dare tangle with God by messing with one of God's chosen? Who would dare even to point a finger? The One who died for us— who was raised to life for us!—is in the presence of God at this very moment sticking up for us. Do you think anyone is going to be able to drive a wedge between us and Christ's love for us? There is no way! Not trouble, not hard

will be able to separate us from the love of God that is in Christ Jesus our Lord.	times, not hatred, not hunger, not homelessness, not bullying threats, not backstabbing, not even the worst sins listed in Scripture:
	They kill us in cold blood because they hate you. We're sitting ducks; they pick us off one by one.
	None of this fazes us because Jesus loves us. I'm absolutely convinced that nothing—nothing living or dead, angelic or demonic, today or tomorrow, high or low, thinkable or unthinkable— absolutely *nothing* can get between us and God's love because of the way that Jesus our Master has embraced us.

Eugene Peterson in *The Message* is simply adding to God's Word to support his theological position. There is not one single verse in the entire Bible that says *nothing* can separate us from Christ. However, there are verses that say there is *nothing* that can separate Christ from us. Think about it **(1)** blaspheme against the Holy Spirit is an unforgivable sin, and it will certainly separate us from Christ. **(2)** Why does Scripture, speaking to those who are saved believers, warn us against "drifting away," "begging off," "turning away," "falling away," "drawing away," becoming sluggish," "becoming hardened by the deceptive power of sin," "tiring out," or "shrinking back to destruction," if it was not possible for something to separate us from Christ. **(3)** Why do the New Testament writers warn us of "false teachers," "divisions," "stumbling other Christians," "temptation," "false prophets," or even "Satan the Devil," if these things are incapable of separating us from Christ? Again, we can be separated from Christ, but there is nothing that can separate Christ from us.

Words and Meaning

The Dynamic Equivalent translator believes that somehow meaning exists apart from words. When asked in an interview for Christianity Today Magazine, "What do you consider your most important contribution to Bible translation?" Eugene A. Nida responded, "To help people be willing to say what the text means, not what the words are, but what the text means." The interviewer goes on to ask, "How did you develop your ideas about Bible translation 50 years ago?" Nida replied:

> When I was at the University of California, Los Angeles, our professors would never let us translate literally. They said, "We want to know the meaning. We don't want to know just the words." I found that a number of the Greek classics had been translated very meaningfully, much better than the Bible had been translated. I thought it a tragedy to have the Scriptures in a form that most people misinterpret. Why should the Bible be so much more poorly translated than secular texts? I studied linguistics, Greek, Latin, and Hebrew, and I decided that we've got to approach the Scripture as though it is the message and try to give its meaning, not just to repeat the words.[32]

---

[32] Nida, Eugene A. "Meaning-full Translations." *Christianity Today*, October 07, 2002: 46-49.

What Nida left out of this discussion is that the goal of every literal translator is to convey the meaning of the Biblical language into the English language. The difference is that they believe this is best accomplished by giving the reader what was said, while Nida and his followers believe that the translator has to go beyond what was said into the realms of translating what is meant by what was said, because "they [you the reader] don't understand the text," so says Nida.

Does the translator seek to render into English what was said in the original language as correspondingly as possible? Take note that an accurate translation is *not* one that is going beyond the English equivalent, in search of rendering the meaning of those words, but is one that seeks to render the *words* of the original language text into the English equivalent (corresponding) word or phrase as *accurately* as possible. A translation is certainly inaccurate if the English edition does not correspond to the original, like a mirror reflection, in any of the following ways:

- if all of the original words are not accounted for by an English equivalent;
- if the translation has added to or taken away from the original in any way (this does not negate the fact that words may need to be added to complete the sense in the English translation);
- Finally, if the meaning that the reader could derive by the corresponding English words has been affected, changed, in any way by an interpretive method.[33]

Roughly, six months after John started preaching, Jesus comes to him at the Jordan. Jesus asks John to baptize him. At once John is in opposition to such an idea: "I have need to be baptized by you, and do you come to me?" Yet, despite John's objection, Jesus insists:

---

[33] These three means of inaccuracy are qualified by the phrase, 'as far as possible.' Certainly, there will be exceptions to the rule.

Matt 3:15 (NU)[34]	Matt 3:15 (LEB)	Matt 3:15 (CEV)
having answered, but the Jesus said to him, "allow now thusly for fitting it is to us to fulfill all rightness" Then he allowed him.	But Jesus answered *and* said to him, "Permit *it* now, for in this way it is right for us to fulfill all righteousness." Then he permitted him.	Jesus answered, "For now this is how it should be, because we must do all that God wants us to do." Then John agreed.

The reader of the Lexham English Bible, ESV, NASB, and RSV will be reading the very words of God as they correspond in English: "to fulfill all righteousness." The reader of the Contemporary English Version will get the interpretation of God's words as, "do all that God wants us to do," which the TEV renders as "*do all that God requires.*" The TEV's interpretation is similar to a number of other dynamic equivalent translations (NEB, NLT, and NIRV). The literal translators give us the corresponding English words of what the Bible says, while the dynamic equivalent translators interpret those very words to mean "obedience," as understood by these translation committees.

What is meant by "permit it now," by "for in this way," by "it is right", or by "for us to fulfill all righteousness"? It is up to each reader of the Bible, to determine what is meant by these words. It is not the job of the translator to interpret what was said, but to give the reader what was said, for interpretation. Just looking at one of the phrases, what is meant by "to fulfill all righteousness"? Is it referring to the doing of all that God

[34] Nestle-Aland 27th edition and United Bible Societies 4th edition Greek Interlinear

asks or requires, in other words, obedience? Does it mean that John and Jesus were righteous individuals? Does it mean, by baptism that Jesus would be entering a path of a right relationship with his Father, a symbol of presenting himself to doing the will of his Father? Again, it is up to the reader to make the determination as to what was meant by the words that Jesus used. Sadly, the reader of the CEV, TEV, and other dynamic equivalent translations do not have that choice, because a committee has made the choice for them.

A Worthy Translation Must Be Clear

The Dynamic Equivalent translators have given a high priority to the quality of being clear in their translation(s). In the process of expressing these worthy goals, they also infer that only the translation philosophy of dynamic equivalence can do this, and to be literal, is to be unclear. In addition, they further infer that the literal translation is willing to sacrifice being clear for the sake of "word worship." These inferences could not be further from the truth. From the first printed translation of William Tyndale (1536) to the present, the goal of literal translations has been to be clear.

> **KJV 1611**: Make it clear when they added any words to make the sense clearer, or to lead to better English syntax ...

> **NKJV**: "... an English text that is both accurate and readable."

> **NASB**: "... a clear and accurate rendering of divinely-revealed truth."

> **ESV**: "... to ensure the fullest accuracy and clarity."

The dynamic equivalent camp would make the argument that to be clear is to be immediately understandable. When they ask if the translation communicates the meaning that the author intended, they are focused on there being absolutely no barriers between the reader and the translation:

- **Idioms:**[35] a land that is "flowing <u>with milk and honey</u>" (ESV) "live in that rich and fertile land" of the (TEV) Deuteronomy 6:3

- **Similes:**[36] "the corpse of Jezebel shall be <u>as dung</u> on the face of the field" (ESV) "Her body will be left to rot on that piece of land." (NIRV) "Jezebel's body will be as waste on the field" (NLV)

- **Metaphors:**[37] "the eyes of Jehovah <u>are in every place</u>." (ASV) "The Lord's eyes see everything" (NCV) Proverbs 15:3

- **Technical Terms:** "Why the Law then? It was added because of transgressions, having been ordained through angels by the agency of a <u>mediator</u>, until the seed would come to whom the promise had been made." (NASB) "What is the use of the Law? It was given later to show that we sin. But it was only supposed to last until the coming of that descendant who was given the promise. In fact, angels gave the Law to Moses, and <u>he</u> gave it to the people." (CEV) Galatians 3:19

---

[35] An idiom is a fixed distinctive expression whose meaning cannot be deduced from the combined meanings of its actual words: "May I get a cup of mud please?" Of course, "mud" is not a cup of wet dirt, but rather a cup of coffee.

[36] A simile is a figure of speech that draws a comparison between two different things, especially a phrase containing the word "like" or ' as," e.g. "as white as a sheet."

[37] A metaphor is an **implicit comparison:** the use to describe somebody or something of a word or phrase that is not meant literally but by means of a vivid comparison expresses something about him, her, or it, e.g. saying that somebody is a snake.

- **Vocabulary Level:** KJV Reading Level (12th) NASB Reading Level (11th) ESV Reading Level (8th) GNT Reading Level (6th) CEV Reading Level (5th) NIRV Reading Level (3rd)

- **Religious Vocabulary:** "to give his life as a ransom for many" (ESV) "will give his life to rescue many people" (CEV) Matthew 20:28

For the thought-for-thought translator, "being clear," means that nothing in the words of their translation is to be difficult to understand. They hold to this concept, even in the face of the Apostle Peter's words about the Apostle Paul's letters: "there are some things in them that are hard to understand." (2 Pet 3:16) Why did Peter find Paul's letters hard to understand? The 27 books of the New Testament were written on different levels. However, one could argue for the most part; they are not literary, and they are not common as a whole, more in the middle. For instance, Paul wrote at times in a literary Koine, as is true of Luke as well. Peter, Mark, and John, on the other hand, wrote on a much lower level. Regardless of this, idioms were still idioms, similes were still similes, metaphors were still metaphors, technical terms were still used, as well as higher levels of vocabulary, and religious terms. Moreover, the King James Version is at a 12th-grade reading level, and it was used for centuries. Are we to believe that our modern world is less intelligent than that of the 17th to the 19th centuries?

Being clear to the Dynamic Equivalent translator also means being transparent (able to see through). In other words, they are simplifying and removing on all levels, to allow today's reader to see through time, and fully grasp what was meant [as per the translator's interpretation], by the words of the original writer to the original reader, as though they were there. This is a fallacy in thinking, as we just learned from Peter, who did not readily understand Paul's letters, even though he was an apostle of the Christian congregation at that time, let alone the lay congregation member of the first-century. Therefore, obviously, it is too much to assume that all the early readers of the Greek New Testament readily understood the text, just because they readily understood the Greek of the day.

For the literal translator, they too see being clear as being transparent (able to see through). However, they work to bring the text to the reader, not the reader to the text. They wish to make the original text transparent to today's reader, by using words that correspond to the original. However, it is much more than bringing the original language words of Hebrew and Greek to the modern reader in a corresponding English word. The Bible is full of idioms like "flowing with milk and honey." The simplest figure of speech is the *simile* ("you are the light of the world"). Though simple, it is very effective. The Bible is rich with metaphors, like "he is like a tree planted by streams of water." The world of the Bible is filled with whole other cultures that span 4,000 years of time, covering a variety of homes, foods and meals, clothing, home life, marriage, health, education, cities, and towns or a nomadic lifestyle, and ways of spending time.

We will look at some scriptural examples, with the purpose of seeing if any of the following three principles are violated,

- If all of the original words are not accounted for by an English equivalent;

- If the translation has added to or taken away from the original in any way;

- Finally, if the meaning that the reader could derive by the corresponding English words has been affected, changed, in any way by an interpretive method.

Literal Translation	Dynamic Equivalent
Corresponding English	**Interpretation of Words**
Psalm 34:5 (UASV) 5 Those who look to him are radiant, and their faces shall never be ashamed.	**Psalm 34:5** (CEV) 5 Keep your eyes on the LORD! You will shine like the sun and never blush with shame.
Psalm 63:11 (UASV) 11 But the king will rejoice in God; everyone who swears by him will exult, for the mouth of those speaking lies will be stopped.	**Psalm 63:11** (CEV) 11 Because of you, our God, the king will celebrate with your faithful followers, but liars will be silent.
Ecclesiastes 9:8 (UASV) 8 Let your garments be always white, and let not oil be lacking on your head.	**Ecclesiastes 9:8** (NLT) 8 Wear fine clothes, with a splash of cologne!
Romans 1:5 (UASV) 5 through whom we have received grace and apostleship for the obedience of faith among all the nations on behalf of his name,	**Romans 1:5** (NCV) 5 Through Christ, God gave me the special work of an apostle, which was to lead people of all nations to believe and obey. I do this work for him.

A Worthy Translation is Consistent

Consistency is of the highest importance when it comes to finding a worthy translation. True the translation does not want to take this principle to the extreme but is has been almost completely removed from the Dynamic Equivalent sense-for-sense translations, and should be considered more in your literal translations as well.

As has been well observed, "There must be consistency in the translation of technical words with a rather sharply fixed content of meaning, not allowing translation to blur the distinctions carried by different words in the original. In the New Testament, there is a distinction between 'Hades' and 'Gehenna.' The former is the Greek equivalent of the Hebrew 'Sheol,' the world of the dead; the latter is the final place of punishment for the wicked."—*Why So Many Bibles*, American Bible Society.

(Interlinear) United Bible Societies Greek New Testament, Fourth Revised Edition, 1993			
Matt 5:22: will be liable to the fire of **Gehenna**	Matt 10:28: can destroy both soul and body in **Gehenna**	Matt 11:23: will be brought down to **Hades**	Matt 16:18: and the gates of **Hades** shall not prevail against it

How do the modern translations perform in reflecting the original language words of Gehenna and Hades? Do they use more than one English word to translate Hades? Do they translate both Gehenna and Hades as "hell"? Those that are consistent are the NIV, NASB, ASV and the HCSB. They translate both Gehenna (5:22; 10:28), as hell, and both Hades (11:23; 16:18), like Hades. Those that are inconsistent are the ESV, translating both Gehenna (5:22; 10:28), as hell, but rendering only 11:23 as Hades, with 16:18 being rendered as hell. The NLT goes even further by translating both Gehenna (5:22; 10:28), as hell, but rendering only 11:23 as 'the place of the dead,' with 16:18 being rendered as hell. Ironically, the forthcoming new translation UASV did the best in this exercise. They translate both Gehenna (5:22; 10:28), as Gehenna, and both Hades (11:23; 16:18), like Hades.

Another example of inconsistency can be found in the translation of *doulos*,[38] a purchased slave, *diakonos*,[39] a servant or minister. The Bible refers to Christians as slaves, as they were bought with the price of Jesus Christ's blood; making them slaves of the heavenly Father and his Son, both being the master over these purchased slaves. A slave of Christ is not to be confused with hired servants, who may choose to quit when they please. The ESV, NASB, NIV, ASV, RSV, TEV CEV all shy away from using the word "slave" as a reference to Christians. However, who are we to set aside the choice of words by the inspired Bible writers, who chose "slave" over "servant." Among the few that have not sidestepped this tough decision are the NLT, UASV, and HSCB. (Rom. 1:1; 1 Cor. 7:23) Either we choose a translation that reflects what was written or a diluted version of what was written, or worse still, we chose an interpretation of what was written.

Repeated Units

Repeated units are one marker or signal that help the exegete (interpreter, us), to determine a book's theme, by recognizing its boundaries and layers between the constituent parts of the whole.

Matthew 5:21-22 Updated American Standard Version (UASV)

[21] "You have heard that it was said to ... [22] But I say to you that

---

[38] William Arndt, Frederick W. Danker and Walter Bauer, *A Greek-English Lexicon of the New Testament and Other Early Christian Literature*, 3rd ed. (Chicago: University of Chicago Press, 2000), 260.

[39] William D. Mounce, *Mounce's Complete Expository Dictionary of Old & New Testament Words* (Grand Rapids, MI: Zondervan, 2006), 632.

Matthew 5:27-28 Updated American Standard Version (UASV)

[27] "You have heard that it was said, 'You shall not commit adultery;'[40] [28] but I say to you that ...

Matthew 5:31-32 Updated American Standard Version (UASV)

[31] "It was said, 'Whoever divorces his wife away, let him give her a certificate of divorce'; [32] but I say to you that everyone who divorces his wife, except on the ground of sexual immorality,[41] ....

Matthew 5:33-34 Updated American Standard Version (UASV)

[33] "Again you have heard that it was said to those of old, 'You shall not swear falsely, but shall perform to the Lord what you have sworn.'[42] [34] But I say to you, Do not swear at all, either by heaven, for it is the throne of God,

Matthew 5:38-39 Updated American Standard Version (UASV)

[38] "You have heard that it was said, 'An eye for an eye, and a tooth for a tooth.'[43] [39] But I say to you, Do not resist the one who is wicked; but whoever slaps you on your right cheek, turn the other to him also.

---

[40] Ex. 20:14; Deut. 5:17

[41] **Sexual Immorality:** (Heb. *zanah*; Gr. *porneia*) A general term for immoral sexual acts of any kind: such as adultery, prostitution, sexual relations between people not married to each other, homosexuality, and bestiality.–Num. 25:1; Deut. 22:21; Matt. 5:32; 1 Cor. 5:1.

[42] A quotation from Lev. 19:12

[43] A quotation from Ex. 21:24; Lev. 24:20

Matthew 5:43-44 Updated American Standard Version (UASV)

[43] "You have heard that it was said, 'You shall love your neighbor[44] and hate your enemy.'[45] [44] But I say to you, love your enemies and pray for those who persecute you,

Matthew 7:28 Updated American Standard Version (UASV)

[28] And it happened when Jesus finished these sayings, the crowds were astounded[46] at his teaching;

Matthew 11:1 Updated American Standard Version (UASV)

[11] When Jesus had finished giving instructions to his twelve disciples, he set out from there to teach and preach in their cities.

Matthew 13:53 Updated American Standard Version (UASV)

[53] When Jesus had finished these parables, He departed from there.

Matthew 19:1 Updated American Standard Version (UASV)

[19] When Jesus had finished saying these things, he departed from Galilee and came into the region of Judea beyond the Jordan;

---

[44] A quotation from Lev. 19:18

[45] A twisting of Deut. 23:3–6

[46] **Astounded:** (Gr. *ekplēssō*) This is one who is extremely astounded or amazed, so much so that they lose their mental self-control, as they are overwhelmed emotionally. – Matt. 7:28; Mark 1:22; 7:37; Lu 2:48; 4:32; 9:43; Ac 13:12.

Matthew 26:1 Updated American Standard Version (UASV)

26 Now when Jesus had finished saying all these things, he said to his disciples:

These markers are far more likely to be lost in the Dynamic Equivalent, sense-for-sense translations, and far less likely to be lost in your literal translations. If lost in translation, their usefulness in helping to determine a book's theme is lost with them. Therefore, you can either use a consistent literal translation or learn to read Hebrew and Greek.

A Worthy Translation is Faithful

What exactly do we mean by faithful, and faithful to what or whom? By faithful, we mean unwavering to the original, to the author himself. However, there are times when translation committees choose to be unfaithful to the original text. Obviously, theological bias should not affect its rendering.

Romans 9:5 (RSV)	Romans 9:5 (NLT)
5 to them belong the patriarchs, and of their race, according to the flesh, is the Christ. God who is over all be blessed forever. Amen.	5 Abraham, Isaac, and Jacob are their ancestors, and Christ himself was an Israelite as far as his human nature is concerned. And he is God, the one who rules over everything and is worthy of eternal praise! Amen.

Romans 9:5: The Revised Standard Version takes *ho on* ["the one who is"] as the opening of a separate, stand-alone sentence or clause that is independent of Christ, which is referring to God (the Father) and pronouncing a blessing upon him for the provisions he made. Here and

in Ps 67:19 in the LXX[47] the predicate *eulogetos* [blessed"] occurs after the subject *Theos* ["God"]. Textual scholar, Bruce M. Metzger made the following point:

> On the other hand, in the opinion of others of the Committee, none of these considerations seemed to be decisive, particularly since nowhere else in his genuine epistles does Paul ever designate ho khristos ["the Christ"] as Theos ["God"]. In fact, on the basis of the general tenor of his theology it was considered tantamount to impossible that Paul would have expressed Christ's greatness by calling him God blessed forever.[48]

A detailed study of the construction in Romans 9:5 is found in *The Authorship of the Fourth Gospel and Other Critical Essays*, by Ezra Abbot, Boston, 1888, pp. 332-438. On pp. 345, 346 and 432 he says:

> "But here *ho on* ["the one who is"] is separated from *ho khristos* ["the Christ"] by to kata *sarka* ["according to the flesh"], which in reading *must* be followed by a pause,—a pause which is lengthened by the special emphasis given to the kata *sarka* ["according to the flesh"] by the *to* ["the"]; and the sentence which precedes is complete in itself grammatically, and requires nothing further logically; for it was only as to the flesh that Christ was from the Jews. On the other hand, as we have seen (p. 334), the enumeration of blessings which immediately precedes, crowned by the inestimable blessing of the advent of Christ, naturally suggests an ascription of praise and thanksgiving to God as

---

[47] Septuagint (Greek translation of the Hebrew Old Testament)

[48] Bruce Manning Metzger and United Bible Societies, *A Textual Commentary on the Greek New Testament, Second Edition a Companion Volume to the United Bible Societies' Greek New Testament (4th Rev. Ed.)* (London; New York: United Bible Societies, 1994), 461-62.

the Being who rules over all; while a doxology is also suggested by the Amen ["Amen"] at the end of the sentence. From every point of view, therefore, the doxological construction seems easy and natural. . . . The naturalness of a pause after *sarka* ["flesh"] is further indicated by the fact that we find a point after this word in all our oldest MSS. that testify in the case,—namely, A, B, C, L, . . . I can now name, besides the uncials A, B, C, L, . . . at least twenty-six cursives which have a stop after *sarka* ["flesh"], the same in general which they have after *aionas* ["forever"] or Amen ["Amen"]."

Therefore, Romans 9:5 in the Revised Standard Version is correct in its ascribing praise and thanksgiving to God (the Father).

> The problem is compounded by the fact that there is practically no punctuation in the ancient manuscripts and we must decide for ourselves whether it is better to put a comma or a full stop after "flesh"; the former ascribes deity to Christ, the latter makes for a doxology to the Father. The grammatical arguments almost all favor the first position, but most recent scholars accept the second on the grounds that Paul nowhere else says explicitly that Christ is God; he may come near it, but, they say, he always stops short of it.[49]

Acts 20:28 (RSV)	Acts 20:28 (NLT)
[28] Take heed to yourselves and to all the flock, in which the Holy Spirit has made you overseers, to	[28] So guard yourselves and God's people. Feed and shepherd God's flock, his church, purchased with his

---

[49] Leon Morris, *The Epistle to the Romans* (Grand Rapids, Mich.; Leicester, England: W.B. Eerdmans; Inter-Varsity Press, 1988), 349.

care for the church of God which he obtained with the blood of his own Son.	own blood, over which the Holy Spirit has appointed you as elders.

Acts 20:28:[50] The RSV reads that the church was purchased with "the blood of his [God's] own Son." On the other hand, the NLT reads that the church was purchased with "God's . . . own blood." Before we can begin determining which of these two renderings is correct, it should be noted that we have two textual problems within this verse. As we are a publication for the lay reader, we will cover the issues, but if any wishes a more technical answer, see *A Textual Commentary on the Greek New Testament* (2nd ed.), by Bruce M. Metzger (1993), or *the New Testament Text and Translation Commentary* by Philip W. Comfort (2008).

Acts 20:28a has three different readings within the Greek New Testament manuscripts: variant (1) "the church of God," variant (2) "the church of the Lord," and variant (3) "the church of the Lord and God." Variant 1 has the better manuscript support and is the choice of the Textus Receptus of 1551, Westcott and Hort text of 1881, the text of Nestle-Aland and the Greek New Testament of the United Bible Society of 1993. The expression "the church of the Lord" is found nowhere in the New Testament. "the church of God" is found eleven times, all by the Apostle Paul, and Luke, the writer of Acts, who was Paul's traveling companion.

The textual criticism principle of what reading led to the other will be discussed in two parts. There is no doubt

---

[50] * J. H. Moulton in A Grammar of New Testament Greek, Vol. 1 (Prolegomena), 1930 ed., p. 90, says: "Before leaving ἴδιος [*idios*] something should be said about the use of ὁ ἴδιος [*ho idios*] without a noun expressed. This occurs in Jn 111 131, Ac 423 2423. In the papyri we find the singular used thus as a term of endearment to near relations . . . . In Expos. VI. iii. 277 I ventured to cite this as a possible encouragement to those (including B. Weiss) who would translate Acts 2028 'the blood of one who was his own.'"

that variant 3 is simply a conflation (combination of variant 1 and variant 2). If "the church of the Lord" is the original reading, it could be that a copyist familiar with Paul made the change to "the church of God." On the other hand, if "the church of God" is the original reading, there is the slight chance that a copyist was influenced by the Greek Old Testament (Septuagint), and changed it to "the church of the Lord."

However, our other principle of textual criticism, 'the more difficult reading is to be preferred' (more difficult to understand), seems to be most helpful. This principle is also related to 'the reading that led to the other,' as the copyist would have moved to an easier reading. The reason being is that it was the tendency of scribes to make difficult readings easier to understand. There is no doubt that "the church of God" is the most difficult reading. Why? The following clause, which will be dealt with shortly could have been taken as "which he purchased with his own blood." This would almost certainly cause pause for any copyist, asking himself, 'does God have blood?' Thus, the original was "the church of God," which was changed to "the church of the Lord," because the idea of saying 'God had blood' would have been repugnant. All things being considered (internal and external evidence), the correct reading is "the church of God."

Acts 20:28b has two different readings within the Greek New Testament Manuscripts:

(1) [literally, the Greek reads "which he purchased with the blood of his own"] "which he [God] purchased with the blood of his own [Son]" or "which he [God] purchased with his own blood" and,

(2) [literally, the Greek reads "which he purchased with the own blood"] "which he purchased with his own blood"

Variant one has the best manuscript evidence by far, and there is no question that it is the original reading. Therefore, we will not use space debating the two but will spend our time determining how it should be understood. Textual scholar Bruce Metzger had this to say,

> This absolute use of ho *idios* ["his Own"] is found in Greek papyri as a term of endearment referring to near relatives. It is possible, therefore, that "his Own" (*ho idios*) was a title that early Christians gave to Jesus, comparable to "the Beloved"; compare Ro 8:32, where Paul refers to God "who did not spare tou idiou huiou ["his own Son"] in a context that clearly alludes to Gn 22:16, where the Septuagint has agapetou huiou ["beloved Son"].

> It may well be, as Lake and Cadbury point out, that after the special meaning of ho *idios* ["his Own"] (discussed in *the previous comment) had dropped out of Christian usage, tou* idiou ["of his own"] of this passage was misunderstood as a qualification of haimatos ("his own blood"). "This misunderstanding led to two changes in the text: *tou haimatos tou idiou* ["the blood of his own"] was changed to *tou idiou haimatos* ["his own blood"] (influenced by Heb. ix. 12?), which is neater but perverts the sense, and *Theou* ["God"] was changed to *kuriou* ["Lord"] by the Western revisers, who doubtless shrank from the implied phrase 'the blood of God.'"[51]

In the end, we must draw the conclusion from all of the evidence; the Revised Standard Version has followed the evidence, with its rendering: "Take heed to yourselves

---

[51] Bruce Manning Metzger and United Bible Societies, *A Textual Commentary on the Greek New Testament, Second Edition a Companion Volume to the United Bible Societies' Greek New Testament (4th Rev. Ed.)* (London; New York: United Bible Societies, 1994), 427.

and to all the flock, in which the Holy Spirit has made you overseers, to care for the church of God which he obtained with the blood of his own Son." On the other hand, it seems that the New Living Translation publisher or committee has allowed theological bias, once again, to blind them from the evidence, as their rendering makes clear: "So guard yourselves and God's people. Feed and shepherd God's flock, his church, purchased with his own blood, over which the Holy Spirit has appointed you as elders. Dr. Robert H. Stein said in a lecture at Southern Baptist Theological Seminary, 'God does not need our help [in translation]. Simply render it as it should be, whether it supports your position or not.'

Another translation that is no longer being used, but can illustrate a lack of faithfulness to the original is Moffatt's *New Translation of the Bible.* Repeatedly he arranges chapters and verses in a way to suit himself in both the Hebrew Scriptures and the Christian Greek Scriptures. Particularly in what he does with the book of Isaiah is open to censure, rearranging the chapters and verses to suit himself. The Dead Sea Scroll of Isaiah, going back, as it does, about a thousand years earlier than the accepted Masoretic text, leaves Dr. Moffatt without any justification whatsoever for such rearranging of Isaiah. This makes it difficult to find certain Bible texts.

A Worthy Translation is Helpful

It is perfectly acceptable to insert words into the translation to complete the sense in the English text. However, this should be done sparingly and very cautiously as one could intentionally or unintentionally misinform the reader. An example of this is found in the Today's English Version, attempting to make what they felt was implied, explicit. At 1 John 3:2 they have replaced "he" with "Christ." However, this has misinformed their readers, as God is the one referred to here not Jesus Christ.

The context of verse 1 and the first part of verse 2 make this clear.

The Bible reader today has a plethora of English translations to choose from and should search for the one that is beneficial to personal study, Bible research, as well as religious services. Numerous translations convey the very word of God (ESV, NASB, ASV, HCSB, and UASV) On the other hand; there are numerous translations that have become very popular because they are easy to read, sound very modern, and are immediately understandable. One must ask themselves, though, if their understanding is, in fact, the correct understanding. However, as we saw from the above examples, the DE also contains many errors by taking too many liberties in their translation principles. Accuracy, dependability, and being clear are best reflected in literal translations, as they are giving the reader what was said, not what one person or a committee feels the author meant by what was said. Any serious Bible student should be interested in getting the Word of God, as opposed to an interpretation of those words. If we want an interpretation, we should buy a commentary. In fact, this is exactly what the Dynamic Equivalent translations are, mini-commentaries.

We are not suggesting that our readers should not possess a Dynamic Equivalent. What we recommend is that for a study of God's Word, use two or three very good literal translations, and two or three very good dynamic equivalents as a sort of quick commentary on Scripture. As to the literal translations, we would recommend the English Standard Version, 2001 (ESV), The Updated New American Standard Bible, 1995 (NASB), the American Standard Version, 1901 (ASV), the Holman Christian Standard Bible, 2003 (HCSB), as well as the forthcoming Updated American Standard Version, 2016 (UASV). As to the dynamic equivalent, we recommend the New Living Translation, 2007 (NLT), the Good News Translation, 1992 (GNT), and the Contemporary English

Version, 1995 (CEV). We would also recommend two translations that are between the dynamic equivalent and the literal translation: The New International Version, 2011 (NIV) and the New English Translation, 2010 (NET).

APPENDIX A The Most Accurate and Faithful Translation Ever to Be Produce and Published Is Coming

UPDATED AMERICAN STANDARD VERSION OF THE HOLY SCRIPTURES

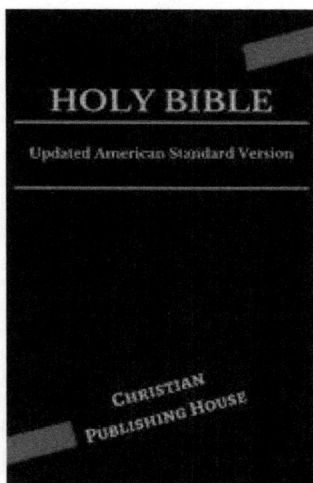

OUR PURPOSE

Our primary purpose is to give the Bible readers what God said by way of his human authors, not what a translator thinks God meant in its place.—Truth Matters!

OUR GOAL

Our primary goal is to be accurate and faithful to the original text. The meaning of a word is the responsibility of the interpreter (i.e., reader), not the translator.—Translating Truth!

Support this Work

http://www.uasvbible.org/donation

Bibliography

Aland, Kurt and Barbara. *The Text of the New Testament.* Grand Rapids: Eerdmans, 1987.

Archer, Gleason L. *A Survey of Old Testament Introduction.* Chicago: Moody, 1994.

—. *Encyclopedia of Bible Difficulties.* Grand Rapids: Zondervan, 1982.

Arduini, Stefano, and Robert Hodgson Jr. *Similarities and Differences in Translation.* New York: American Bible Society, 2004.

Arndt, William, Frederick W. Danker, and Walter Bauer. *A Greek-English Lexicon of the New Testament and Other Early Christian Literature. 3rd ed. .* Chicago: University of Chicago Press, 2000.

Baer, Daniel. *The Unquenchable Fire.* Maitland, FL: Xulon Press, 2007.

Barnett, Paul. *The Birth of Christianity: The First Twenty Years (After Jesus, Vol. 1) .* Grand Rapids, MI: Wm. B. Eerdmans , 2005.

Barnwell, Katharine. *Bible Translation: An Introductory Course in Translation Principles.* Kenya: SIL International, 1975.

—. *Introduction to Semantics and Translation.* England: SIL, 1974.

Beekman, John, and John Callow. *Translating the Word of God.* Grand Rapids: Zondervan, 1974.

Bercot, David W. *A Dictionary of Early Christian Beliefs.* Peabody: Hendrickson, 1998.

Bock, Darrell L. *The Missing Gospels: Unerthing the Truth Behind Alternative Christianities.* Nashville, TN: Thomas Nelson, 2006.

Bock, Darrell L, and Daniel B Wallace. *Dethroning Jesus: Exposing Popular Culture's Quest to Unseat the Biblical Christ.* Nashville: Thomas Nelson, 2007.

Brand, Chad, Charles Draper, and England Archie. *Holman Illustrated Bible Dictionary: Revised, Updated and Expanded.* Nashville, TN: Holman, 2003.

Bruce, F. F. *The New Testament Documents: Are they Reliable?* Downer Groves: Inter Varsity, 1981.

Bruce, F. F., J. I. Packer, Philip Cmfort, and Carl F. H. Henry. *The Origin of the Bible.* Carol Steam, IL: Tyndale House, 1992, 2003.

Comfort, Philip. *Encounterring the Manuscripts: An Introduction to New Testament Paleography and Textual Criticism.* Nashville: Broadman & Holman, 2005.

Comfort, Philip W. *Essential Guide to Bible Versions.* Wheaton: Tyndale House, 2000.

Comfort, Philip W. *New Testament Text and Translation Commentary.* Carol Stream: Tyndale House Publishers, 2008.

Comfort, Philip Wesley. *The Quest for the Original Text of the New Testament.* Eugene: Wipf and Stock, 1992.

Comfort, Philip, and David Barret. *The Text of the Earliest New Testament Greek Manuscripts.* Wheaton: Tyndale House Publishers, 2001.

Cruse, C. F. *Eusebius' Eccliatical History.* Peabody, MA: Hendrickson, 1998.

Dever, William G. *What Did the Biblical Writers Know, and When Did They Know It?* Grand Rapids: William B. Eerdmans Publishing Company, 2001.

Dewey, David. *A User's Guide to Bible Translation: Making the Most of Different Versions.* Downers Grove : InterVaristy Press, 2004.

Durant, Will & Ariel. *The Story of Civilization: Part IV— The Age of Faith.* New York, NY: Simon & Schuster, 1950.

Edwards, Tyron. *A Dictionary of Thoughts.* Detroit: F. B. Dickerson Company, 1908.

Ehrman, Bart D. *Misquoting Jesus: The Story Behind Who Changed the Bible and Why.* New York: Harper One, 2005.

Ehrman, Bart D. Holmes, Michael W. *The Text of the New Testament in Contemporary Research: Essays on the Status Quaestionis .* Grand Rapids, MI: Eerdmans, 1995.

Ehrman, Bart D. *Lost Christianities: The Battles for Scripture and the Faiths We Never Knew .* New York: Oxford University Press, 2003.

Elwell, Walter A. *Evangelical Dictionary of Theology (Second Edition).* Grand Rapids: Baker Academic, 2001.

Elwell, Walter A, and Philip Wesley Comfort. *Tyndale Bible Dictionary.* Wheaton, Ill: Tyndale House Publishers, 2001.

Evans, Craig A. *Fabricating Jesus: How Modern Scholars Distort the Gospels.* Downers Grove, IL: InterVaristy Press, 2002.

F. Garcia Martinez, Julio Barrera, Trebolle, Florentino Garcia Martinez, and J. Trebolle Barrera. *The People of the Dead Sea Scrolls: Their Writings, Beliefs and Practices.* Leiden: Brill Academic, 1995.

Geisler, Norman L. *A Popular Survey of the New Testament.* Grand Rapids: Baker Books, 2007.

—. *Defending Inerrancy: Affirming the Accuracy of Scripture for a New Generation.* Grand Rapids, MI: Baker Books, 2012.

—. *Inerrancy.* Grand Rapids, MI: Zondervan, 1980.

Geisler, Norman L, and William E Nix. *A General Introduction to the Bible.* Chicago: Moody Press, 1996.

Geisler, Norman L. *Biblical Errancy: An Analysis of Its Philosophical Roots.* Eugene, OR: Wipf and Stock Publisher, 1981.

Geisler, Norman L., and Thomas Howe. *The Big Book of Bible Difficulties.* Grand Rapids: Baker Books, 1992.

Green, Joel B, Scot McKnight, and Howard Marshall. *Dictionary of Jesus and the Gospels.* Downers Grove, IL: InterVarsity Press, 1992.

Greenlee, J Harold. *Introduction to New Testament Textual Criticism.* Peabody: Hendrickson, 1995.

Grudem, Wayne, Leland Ryken, John C Collins, Vern S Poythress, and Bruce Winter. *Translating Truth: The Case for Essentially Literal Bible Translation.* Wheaton: Crossway Books, 2005.

Hoffman, Joel M. *AND GOD SAID: How Translations Conceal the Bible's Original Meaning.* New York, NY: Thomas Dunne Books, 2007.

Holmes, Michael W. *The Apostolic Fathers: Greek Texts and English Translations.* Grand Rapids: Baker Academics, 2007.

Hurtado, Larry W. *The Earliest Christian Artifacts: Manuscripts and Christian Origins.* Grand Rapids: Eerdmans, 2006.

James, M R. *The Apocryphal New Testament.* Berkeley, CA: Apocryphile Press, 1924, 2004.

Jones, Timothy Paul. *Misquoting Truth: A Guide to the Fallacies of Bart Ehrman's Misquoting Jesus.* Downer Groves: InterVarsity Press, 2007.

Kaiser, Walter C, Peter H Davids, and Frederick Fyvie , Brauch, Manfred T Bruce. *Hard Sayings of the Bible.* Downer Groves, IL: Inter Varsity Press, 1996.

Keener, Craig S. *The IVP Bible Background Commentary: New Testament.* Downer Groves, IL: InterVarsity Press, 1993.

Kenyon, F. G. *The Palaeography of Greek Papyri.* Whitefish: Kessinger Publishing, 2006.

Kistemaker, Simon J, and William Hendriksen. *New Testament Commentary: Exposition of the Acts of the Apostles .* Grand Rapids, MI: Baker Book House, 1953-2001.

Komoszewski, J. Ed, James M. Sawyer, and Daniel Wallace. *Reinventing Jesus .* Grand Rapids, MI: Kregel Publications, 2006.

Lightfoot, Neil R. *How We Got the Bible.* Grand Rapids, MI: Baker Books, 1963, 1988, 2003.

Lindsell, Harold. *The Battle for the Bible.* Grand Rapids: Zondervan, 1976.

Linnemann. *Is There A Synoptic Problem? Rethinking the Literary Dependance of the First Three Gospels.* Grand Rapids, MI: Baker Book House, 1992.

Linnemann, Eta. *Biblical Criticism on Trial: How Scientific is "Scientific Theology"?* Grand Rapids: Kregel, 2001.

McDonald, Lee Martin. *Forgotten Scriptures: The Selection and Rejection of Early Religious Writings.* Louisville: Westminster John Knox Press , July 13, 2009.

Metzger, Bruce M. *The Text of the New Testament: Its Transmission, Corruption, and Transmission.* New York: Oxford University Press, 1964, 1968, 1992.

Metzger, Bruce M. *A Textual Commentary on the Greek New Testament.* New York: United Bible Society, 1994.

Metzger, Bruce M., and Bart D. Ehrman. *The Text of the New Testament: Its Transmission, Corruption, and Restoration (4th Edition).* New York: Oxford University Press, 2005.

Metzger, Bruce. *The Bible in Translation: Ancient and English Versions.* Grand Rapids: Baker Academic, 2001.

Milligan, George. *The New Testament Documents, Their Origin and Early History* . New York, NY: General Books LLC, 2009.

Mounce, William D. *Mounce's Complete Expository Dictionary of Old & New Testament Words.* Grand Rapids, MI: Zondervan, 2006.

Munday, Jeremy. *Introducing Translation Studies: Theories and Applications (2bd Edition).* London: Routledge, 2009.

Oates, John F., Alan E. Samuel, and Bradford C. Welles. *Yale Papyri in the Beinecke Rare Book and Manuscript Library* . (New Haven: American Society of Papyrologists, 1967.

Orchard, Bernard. *J. J. Griesbach: Synoptic and Text - Critical Studies* . Cambridge: Cambridge University Press, 1776-1976, 2005.

Packer, J. I. *God Speaks to Man: Revelation and the Bible.* Atlanta: Westminster Press, 1965.

Pagels, Elaine. *The Gnostic Gospels.* New York: Vintage, 1989.

Parker, David C. *The living Text of the Gospels.* Cambridge: Cambridge University Press, 1997.

Porter, Stanley E, and Mark J Boda. *Translating the New Testament.* Grand Rapids, MI: Wm. B. Eerdmans, 2009.

Porter, Stanley E, and Richard S Hess. *Translating the Bible: Problems and Prospects.* New York, NY: T&T Clark International, 2004.

Poythress, Vern S. Grudem, Wayne A. *The TNIV and The Gender-Neutral Bible Controversy.* Nashville: Boardman & Holman, 2004.

Price, Randall. *Searching for the Original Bible.* Eugene: Harvest House, 2007.

Ray, Vernon. "The Formal vs Dynamic Equivalent Principle in New Testament Translation." *Restoration Quarterly 25*, 1982: 46-56.

Rhodes, Ron. *The Complete Guid to Bible Translations.* Eugene, OR: Harvest House, 2009.

Richards, E. Randolph. *Paul And First-Century Letter Writing: Secretaries, Composition and Collection.* Downers Grove: InterVarsity Press, 2004.

Roberts, Alexander, and James Donaldson. *The Ante-Nicene Fathers.* Peabody: Hendrickson, 1994.

Roberts, C. H. *Books in the Graeco-Roman World and in the New Testament in the Cambridge History of the Bible, Vol. 1, From the Beginnings to Jerome .* Cambridge: Cambridge University Press, 1970.

Roberts, Colin H. *Manuscript, Society, and Belief in Early Christian Egypt.* London: Oxford University Press, 1979.

Roberts, Colin H., and Theodore C. Skeat. *The Birth of the Codex.* London: Oxford University Press, 1987.

Robertson, A. T. *An Introduction to the Textual Criticism of the New Testament*. London: Hodder & Stoughton, 1925.

Ryken, Leland. *Choosing a Bible: Understanding Bible Translation Differences*. Wheaton: Crossway Books, 2005.

—. *The Word of God in English*. Wheaton: Crossway Books, 2002.

—. *Understanding English Bible Translation: The Case for an Essentially Literal Approach*. Wheaton, IL: Crossway Books, 2009.

Scorgie, Glen G, Mark L Strauss, and Stephen M Voth. *The Challenge of Bible Translation*. Grand Rapids: Zondervan, 2003.

Souter, Alexander. *The Text and Canon of the New Testament*. New York: Charles Scribner's Sons, 1913.

Thomas, Robert L. *How to Choose a Bible Version*. Scotland: Christian Focus Publications, 2000.

—. *Three Views of the Origins of the Synoptic Gospels*. Grand Rapids, MI: Kregel, 2002.

Thomas, Robert L., and F. David Farnell. *THE JESUS CRISIS: The Inroads of Historical Criticism in Evagelical Scholarship*. Grand Rapids, MI: Kregel Publications, 1998.

Torrey, Reuben Archer. *Difficulties in the Bible: Alleged Errors and Contradictions*. Chicago: Moody Press, 1907.

University, Stanford. *Calculating the Time and Cost of Paul's Missionary Journeys*. 2012. http://www.openbible.info/blog/2012/07/calcula ting-the-time-and-cost-of-pauls-missionary-journeys/ (accessed 07 12, 2014).

Vine, W E. *Vine's Expository Dictionary of Old and New Testament Words.* Nashville: Thomas Nelson, 1996.

Virkler, Henry A, and Karelynne Gerber Ayayo. *Hermeneutics: Principles and Processes of Biblical Interpretation.* Grand Rapids, MI: Baker Academic, 1981, 2007.

Wallace, Daniel B. *bible.org.* Winter 2008. http://bible.org/article/number-textual-variants-evangelical-miscalculation (accessed December 18, 2011).

—. *Revisiting the Corruption of the New Testament: Manuscript, Patristic, and Apocryphal Evidence.* Grand Rapids, MI: Kregel Publications, 2011.

Wallace, Daniel. *The Reliability of the New Testament: Bart Ehrman and Daniel Wallace in Dialogue.* Minneapolis, MN: Fortress Press, 2011.

Walton, John H., Victor H. Matthews, and Mark W Chavalas. *The IVP Bible Background Commentary: Old Testament.* Downers Grove: IVP Academic, 2000.

Wegner, Paul D. *A Student's Guide to Textual Criticism of the Bible: Its History Methods & Results.* Downers Grove: InterVarsity Press, 2006.

Westcott, B. F., and Hort F. J. A. *The New Testament in the Original Greek, Vol. 2: Introduction, Appendix.* London: Macmillan and Co., 1882.